# The My Little Pony G1 Collector's Inventory

an unofficial full color illustrated collector's price guide to the first generation of MLP including all US ponies, playsets and accessories released before 1997

by
## Summer Hayes

Priced Nostalgia Press ~ New Jersey

All rights reserved. With the exception of quoting brief passages for the purposes of review, no part of this publication may be reproduced without prior written permission from the publisher. Any reproduction of this work without permission of the publisher is prohibited.

The information in this book is true and complete to the best of our knowledge. All information is offered without any guarantee on the part of the author or publisher, who also disclaim any liability incurred in connection with the use of this guide.

We recognize that My Little Pony and all pony, set, and playset names are the exclusive property of Hasbro, Inc. and are used without permission. We are using them for identification purposes only. This is not an official publication, nor is it affiliated with Hasbro in any way. The toys featured in this book are from the private collection of the author and other collectors.

Additional copies of this book are available at www.PricedNostalgia.com.

**Library of Congress Control Number: 2008925351**

Hayes, Summer. The My Little Pony G1 Collector's Inventory: an unofficial full color illustrated collector's price guide to the first generation of My Little Pony toys including all ponies, playsets and accessories released before 1997. 1st ed. New Jersey: Priced Nostalgia Press, 2008.

ISBN-10: 0978606310
ISBN-13: 9780978606312

Copyright 2008 Priced Nostalgia

All photographs in this guide were taken by Summer Hayes of items in her private collection unless otherwise indicated below.

**Additional Photo Credits**

While I took the majority of the photos in this guide, the following people graciously donated photographs for this gigantic project and I am truly grateful to each and every one of them! Annie Msson donated a picture of Glider. Julie "MustBeJewel" Watts supplied photos of Windsweeper, Song Rider, and the missing Lavender Dream Castle accessories. Jen Oakes donated pictures of Circle Dancer, Mayfair, Colorglow, and Fair Flyer. Caitlin Beam provided a photo of the Dreamy Siamese set. Amanda Lamm-Feltman gave a picture of MOC Adorable Angora. Sheena "Roogna" McNeil donated pictures of missing Twinkle Petites, missing Glowing Magic Petites, Misty, Whinny Winks Inn, and the Petite Pony Ice Cream Shoppe. Julie "BridgetsMum" Alexander supplied photos of Cutie Calico kitten, Happy Hopper, and Scrub-A-Dub Spaniels puppy. Becki Graham (twinkle_pony) donated pictures of Slumber Time Siamese and Sudsy Angoras. Thank you also to Amber (Fire Muse) Dudley for the photo of the prom queen perfume and pony bride ring, Sarah Amos for the photo of the Birds and Flowers Pretty Up and Desiree Skylark for the photo of My Pretty Pony's accessories. Melinda (Baby Starbow MLP) Bruner photographed the Bridal Beauty ring, Debra Birge donated a photo of the Make-up fashion tote and the peach My Pretty Pony accessories photo comes courtesy of Angelika Mühleisen. Special thanks also goes to Angie Gouge (ashylne) who went above and beyond what I asked and provided numerous accessory pictures, missing plush pictures, photos of her gorgeous year three Sea Ponies with their shells, and provided all of the photos for the sticker section from her amazing sticker collection! Thank you all so very much!

# Foreword by Kim Shriner

In the 1980s, My Little Pony was a household name. Children of the 80s in particular are likely to remember the brightly colored hair and unique rump symbols that were the hallmark of My Little Pony, whether they encountered them in stores, at a friend's house or in their toy box. For some people, My Little Pony meant opening a birthday gift and receiving just the one they wanted. For others, who either never had a My Little Pony at all or never had that one special pony, it's an afterimage of a favorite pony and that same desire to have it though their childhood may be far behind. But it is those that find themselves walking through an antique shop years later, spotting out a certain pony and recalling with delight, "I had that one!" that have the desire to once again put a face and name to the pony in front of them. For those, My Little Pony is more than a wildly popular toy line, but rather is like connecting with a long lost childhood friend.

A lot has changed in these last two decades and for My Little Pony fans, that is a good thing. In the 1980s, I knew no one else who was a collector and, as I got older, it was unusual for older kids and adults to be seen playing with little ponies. But today I look around and see teenagers in T-Shirts featuring characters that were first popular many years before they were born and parents sharing the toys that they grew up with their own children.

When I first launched the Dream Valley website in 1997, it was with the hope of not only sharing my knowledge and love of My Little Pony with a newly-forming community, but also to give fans and collectors the opportunity to realize they were not alone in their love of these little ponies. I felt like I was providing a chance for people to rediscover a part of their lives that may have been forgotten. Time and again, I hear from collectors who have brought their old ponies out of storage or have gone to great lengths to replace the ponies they once had and I get many 'thank yous' for being a part of that rediscovery.

In 2005, I attended my first My Little Pony Fair Collector's Convention, something I would have never dreamed of in 1997 and something I definitely wouldn't have even thought possible back in the 80s. I'm both proud and in awe of the community I feel like I have helped create, online and off, not only because it has brought about a new admiration for these little ponies, but because it's brought people who share a common interest together who otherwise may have never met or found a place in which they belong.

My first pony was Cotton Candy; my sister's was Butterscotch. Twenty-five years later, both ponies have a place of honor at the very top of my collection now numbering hundreds. But it's not just about numbers. One of the reasons my memories of My Little Pony are so fond and so important is because they are part of my childhood, like so many other things that were a part of that most impressionable time in my life. It's a time when innocence allows the things we love to be anything we want them to be and so much of the joy surrounding them comes from our own interpretations and imagination.

As our lives change, it's essential that we hold onto these memories and, more importantly, that innocence. Just as I've shared my life with Applejack, Firefly, Peachy, and of course Cotton Candy and look back with happy memories, I look forward to the future of My Little Pony and how this generation of collectors will remember growing up with Pinkie Pie, Rainbow Dash, Star Catcher and all the other ponies currently in stores. Every toy has a memory attached and it is the truly special toys that make a lasting impression.

My Little Pony has successfully entranced three generations already, with no sign of slowing. For My Little Pony collectors, the casual and the serious, each time we find another pony that we were seeking, it rekindles that special connection. A flea market find can feel like a childhood birthday gift, the thrill of a winning auction bid is like the thrill of finding a favorite playmate that had been lost to under your bed and finally getting that pony you wanted most is like seeing that brand new toy on the shelf that you just had to have. This is why, for many of us, My Little Pony will always be so much more than just a toy.

As you peruse the ponies on these pages and take your own journey into the world of My Little Pony, just remember that wherever life takes you, the ponies will all be waiting with cheerful colors, familiar symbols, and sweet smiles... at the end of the rainbow.

**Kimberly Shriner** is the creator of *Dream Valley: a Collector's Guide to My Little Pony* (http://www.kimsites.net/dreamvalley), one of the first and largest My Little Pony websites. She is also the author of the *Oak Branch Woods* series of nature-inspired novels (http://www.kimsites.net/obw)

# Introduction

In 1982, Hasbro released a set of six basic ponies in pastel colors, each with a brushable mane and tail, whimsical name, and a distinguishing rump design to identify them by. Though relatively simple compared to other toys of the 1980s, My Little Pony struck a chord with little girls everywhere. Those original six ponies soon expanded into hundreds of different sets of ponies forming not only one of the most popular and successful toy lines of the 1980s, but also one that continues its popularity to this day. From those original six, My Little Pony expanded into a world where unicorns, pegasus, sea, and flutter ponies all lived, worked and played together in the mythical Dream Valley. This pony world fueled 10 successful years of MLP toys and gave rise to two television specials, two different cartoon series and a major motion picture, *My Little Pony: The Movie*.

My Little Pony toys enjoyed a successful run in the United States for ten years, from 1982 to 1992, with hundreds of items released for sale. To the delight of My Little Pony fans, Hasbro bought My Little Pony back for a second generation in the late 1990s, and for a third generation in 2003. This third generation continues with new pony items, movies and more to this day and has brought the world of MLP to a whole new generation.

As we mark the 25th Anniversary of Hasbro's My Little Pony brand in 2008, adults and children alike continue to play with and collect these enchanting toys. But as the world of My Little Pony continues to expand as well as age, fans and collectors find themselves with new challenges in tracking down missing and wanted items, identifying the value of their collection, and matching accessories to their ponies.

My grandfather gave me my first pony, Applejack, at a very young age. I was smitten with the little orange pony and with the help of my parents, grandparents, aunts, and uncles, Applejack quickly found herself surrounded by many other My Little Ponies. As each new pony joined my growing collection, I took special care to memorize her name and would place her carefully among the others.

After the original run of My Little Pony came to an end, I continued to add to my collection through garage sales and flea markets and, eventually, online. In 1999, I began compiling notes on ponies and pony accessories using photos of mint on card ponies from online auctions, from my own collection, and from the collections of friends. It was my goal that someday I would create a complete resource containing all My Little Ponies, playsets, and accessories to share with fellow collectors. Nearly nine years after I began this project, it is finally complete and ready to share.

The My Little Ponies in this book are organized according to the year and set in which they were released. Playsets, Mail Order and Special Offers, Petite Ponies, Dream Beauties, and other sets are listed in separate sections.

A pony name index is provided in the back of this guide to assist the reader when searching for a specific pony. This book contains My Little Ponies, playsets, accessories, and related lines available in the US from 1981 to 1992.

I hope that you will find this guide helpful while identifying My Little Ponies, organizing your collection, or creating your My Little Pony wish list. For additions, corrections, price guide updates or other information about anything in this book, please visit my website at http://www.purplepajamapress.com.

## About the Author

**Summer Hayes** has been a My Little Pony Collector for over twenty years. Her love of ponies started at a very early age and continued into her adult life. Over the years, she has accumulated an extensive collection of ponies, accessories, and merchandise from all three generations and from multiple countries. Summer has been active in the My Little Pony collecting community for many years and has attended pony meets and conventions throughout the country. Summer hosted *My Little Pony Celebration: A Midwest Pony Meet* in Greenville, Indiana in the summer of 2002 and co-hosted the event in Lafayette, Indiana in the summer of 2005. Summer is an elementary teacher and currently resides with her husband, Matthew, in Roanoke, Virginia. She is also the author of the *The My Little Pony G3 Collector's Inventory* as well as an upcoming illustrated price guide to My Little Pony G2.

# Table of Contents

**Understanding the Price Guide** ............................................. 10
**How to Identify a Real My Little Pony from a Fake** .......... 11
**Recurring Accessories** ............................................................. 12
**My Pretty Pony** ........................................................................ 17
**1982-1983 Year 1** .................................................................... **19**
    Original Ponies ........................................................................ 20
**1983-1984 Year 2** .................................................................... **21**
    Earth Ponies ............................................................................ 22
    Unicorn and Pegasus Ponies .................................................. 23
    Rainbow Ponies ....................................................................... 24
    Sea Ponies ................................................................................ 25
**1984-1985 Year 3** .................................................................... **27**
    Earth Ponies (second set) ....................................................... 28
    Unicorns and Pegasus (second set) ........................................ 29
    Megan and Sundance .............................................................. 30
    Rainbow Ponies (second set) .................................................. 31
    Baby Ponies ............................................................................. 32
    Baby Sea Ponies ...................................................................... 35
    "Ember's Dream" .................................................................... 36
**1985-1986 Year 4** .................................................................... **37**
    So-Soft Ponies ......................................................................... 38
    Baby Pony with Beddy Bye Eyes ........................................... 41
    Twinkle Eyed .......................................................................... 43
    Megan & So-Soft Sundance ................................................... 44
    Flutter Ponies .......................................................................... 45
    Pretty 'n Pearly Baby Sea Ponies ........................................... 46
    Party Gift Pack ........................................................................ 47
    Molly & Baby Sundance ........................................................ 49
**1986-1987 Year 5** .................................................................... **51**
    Baby Ponies with First Tooth ................................................. 52
    Big Brother Ponies .................................................................. 54
    Flutter Ponies (second set) ...................................................... 55
    Pony Friends ............................................................................ 56
    Newborn Twins ....................................................................... 57
    Princess Ponies with Bushwoolies .......................................... 59
    Sea Sparkle Baby Sea Ponies ................................................. 61
    So-Soft Ponies (second set) .................................................... 62
    Slumber Party Gift Pack ......................................................... 63
    Soft and Sleepy Newborns ...................................................... 64
    Twinkle Eyed Ponies (second set) .......................................... 66
    Twice As Fancy Ponies ........................................................... 67

## 1987-1988 Year 6 — 69

- Big Brother Ponies (second set) — 70
- Brush 'n Grow Ponies — 71
- Happy Tails Ponies — 72
- Magic Message Ponies — 74
- Newborn Twins (second set) — 75
- Peek-A-Boo Baby Ponies — 77
- Pony Friends (second set) — 78
- Princess Ponies (second set) — 79
- Summer Wing Ponies — 80
- Sundae Best Ponies — 82
- Sweetberry Ponies — 83
- Twice-As-Fancy Ponies (second set) — 84
- Watercolor Baby Sea Ponies — 85

## 1988-1989 Year 7 — 87

- Baby Fancy Pants Ponies — 88
- Baby Ponies & Pretty Pals — 89
- Candy Cane Ponies — 91
- Dance 'n Prance Ponies — 92
- Loving Family Ponies — 94
- Megan & Twice As Fancy Sundance — 95
- Merry-Go-Round Ponies — 96
- Newborn Ponies — 97
- Perfume Puff Ponies — 98
- Playtime Baby Brother Ponies — 99
- Princess Brush 'n Grow Ponies — 101
- Sparkle Ponies — 102
- Sunshine Ponies — 103
- Sweetheart Sister Ponies — 105
- Windy Wing Ponies — 106

## 1989-1990 Year 8 — 109

- Baby Sparkle Ponies — 110
- The Christmas Pony — 110
- Baby Drink 'n Wet Ponies — 111
- Glitter Sweetheart Sister Ponies — 112
- Pony Bride — 113
- Prom Queen Sweetheart Sister Ponies — 113
- Rainbow Curl Ponies — 115
- Sweetsteps Ballerina Ponies — 116
- Tropical Ponies — 117

## 1990-1991 Year 9 — 119

- Baby Ballerina Ponies — 120
- Baby Rainbow Ponies — 121

    Firefly's Adventure ............................................................................................... 121
    Glow 'n Show Ponies ........................................................................................... 122
    Precious Pocket Ponies ......................................................................................... 123
    Pretty Ponies ........................................................................................................ 124
    Princess Ponies (third set) .................................................................................... 125
    Rockin' Beat Ponies ............................................................................................. 125
    Secret Surprise Ponies ......................................................................................... 126
    Teeny Tiny Ponies ............................................................................................... 128

## 1991-1992 Year 10 .................................................................................................. 129
    Birthday Pony ..................................................................................................... 130
    Bridal Beauty ....................................................................................................... 130
    Colorswirl Ponies ................................................................................................. 131
    Fancy Mermaid Ponies ........................................................................................ 132
    Flower Fantasy Ponies ......................................................................................... 133
    Paradise Baby Ponies ........................................................................................... 134
    Soda Sippin' Ponies ............................................................................................. 135
    Sundazzle Ponies ................................................................................................. 136
    Sweet Kisses Ponies ............................................................................................. 137
    Teeny Pony Twins ............................................................................................... 138
    Sweet Talkin' Ponies ........................................................................................... 139

## Petite Ponies ........................................................................................................... 141
    Pony Parade ........................................................................................................ 142
    Sparkle Ponies ..................................................................................................... 142
    Pretty 'n Pearly ................................................................................................... 143
    Ponytail Petites .................................................................................................... 144
    Twinkle Ponies .................................................................................................... 145
    Bright Sight ......................................................................................................... 146
    Glowing Magic .................................................................................................... 147
    Petite Pony Homes .............................................................................................. 148
    Petite Pony Shoppes ............................................................................................ 150
    Prancing Pretty Carousel ..................................................................................... 151
    Royal Pony Palace ............................................................................................... 151

## Dream Beauties ..................................................................................................... 155
    Highflying Beauties ............................................................................................. 156
    Rainbow Beauties ................................................................................................ 157
    Shimmering Beauties .......................................................................................... 158
    Showtime Beauties .............................................................................................. 159
    Sweet Perfume Beauties ...................................................................................... 159
    Trim 'n Grow Beauties ........................................................................................ 160

## Li'l Litters and Nursery Families ........................................................................ 163
    Li'l Litters ............................................................................................................ 164
    My Little Puppy Li'l Litters ................................................................................. 164
    My Little Kitty Li'l Litters ................................................................................... 165

    My Little Bunny Li'l Litters ......... 166
    Nursery Families ......... 167
    My Little Puppy Nursery Families ......... 167
    My Little Kitty Nursery Families ......... 168

**Plush Ponies** ......... **169**

**Playsets** ......... **175**
    Pretty Parlor ......... 176
    Show Stable ......... 177
    Waterfall ......... 178
    Dream Castle ......... 179
    Baby Buggy ......... 180
    Megan's Place ......... 181
    Lullabye Nursery ......... 182
    Pony Purse ......... 183
    Baby Bonnet School of Dance ......... 184
    Paradise Estate ......... 185
    Pony Purse (second set) ......... 187
    Satin Slipper Sweet Shoppe ......... 187
    Perm Shoppe ......... 188
    Poof 'n Puff Perfume Palace ......... 189
    Brush Me Beautiful Boutique ......... 191
    Rock-a-Bye Bed ......... 192
    Scrub-a-Dub Tub ......... 193
    Sweet Dreams Crib ......... 193
    Home Sweet Home ......... 194
    Dream Castle (second edition) ......... 195
    Princess Baby Buggy ......... 196
    Pony and Accessory Cases ......... 197

**Mail Order and Special Offer Ponies** ......... **199**
    Ember, My Beautiful Baby Pony ......... 200
    Birthflower Ponies ......... 200
    Li'l Tot Pony ......... 202
    Collector Ponies ......... 202
    Hollywood and Spike ......... 203
    Stockings, the Holiday Pony ......... 204
    Wedding Ponies ......... 204
    Blue Ribbon ......... 206
    Sparkle Ponies ......... 207
    Clipper ......... 208
    Pretty Mane Ponies ......... 209
    Baby Sisters ......... 209
    Baby Pearlized Ponies ......... 210
    Baby Birthday Ponies ......... 211

| | |
|---|---|
| Playset Ponies | 211 |
| Make-Up and Fashion Tote | 212 |
| Mommy Charms | 214 |
| Fan Club Mommy Charm | 215 |
| McDonald's Bookmarks | 216 |
| Pony and Pendant Pair | 216 |
| Goldilocks | 217 |
| Rapunzel | 217 |
| Valentine's Day Baby Ponies | 218 |
| Mommy and Baby Pony Set | 218 |
| Chuck E. Cheese Baby Pony | 219 |
| Christmas Baby Pony | 219 |
| **Pony Wear** | **220** |
| Pony Wear with Jewelry | 223 |
| Mother and Baby Wear | 224 |
| Baby Pony Wear with Pocket Pals | 227 |
| Megan and Pony Wear | 229 |
| Play 'n Wear | 231 |
| Costume Wear | 232 |
| Pretty Ups | 234 |
| **Stickers** | **236** |
| 1983-1984 Stickers | 236 |
| 1984-1985 Stickers | 237 |
| 1985-1986 Stickers | 240 |
| **Other Licensed Merchandise** | **246** |

# Understanding the Price Guide

The prices listed in this book are for loose ponies in mint condition without accessories. Prices for each pony will decrease based on any flaws as described below.

**Mint condition** is defined as ponies outside of their packages which DO NOT have any of the following:
- Cut or frizzy (crunchy) hair, balding, or missing hair plugs or tail.
- Marks on their body that cannot be removed (such as pen, marker, etc).
- Discoloration of body or brown age spots.
- Holes, tears, scratches or other wear to body or head
- Damage, wear or breakage to the symbol or special feature of that set. For example, a So-Soft pony with balding could not be considered mint just as a Happy Tails Pony whose tail no longer spins could not be considered mint. Examples of these types of damage will be covered in greater detail on individual set pages.

**Collector's Note:** Two very common MLP flaws that are easy to miss, but important to mention are as follows. Some collectors do not care about these as they are not cosmetic but some do.
- **Does your pony's head turn?** Only ball jointed heads (Peek-a-Boo and Playtime Baby Brother sets) or poseable ponies (Sweetsteps and Baby Ballerina sets) are meant to have heads that turn. If any other pony head style can turn its head, this means that the connectors on the base of its head are torn.
- **Is there a rattle noise when you shake your pony?** If so, this is caused by the pony's tail having been pulled out at some point, causing the washer at the base of the tail to become loose.

A pony with extreme damage that is beyond repair is called **custom bait** or just **bait** for short. These ponies still have value to those that like to create custom MLP creations which usually entails repainting the pony and re-rooting hair. The value of these ponies is low unless the pony was rare to begin with. Big Brother ponies and other uncommon molds are worth more even as bait than the more common molds.

In most cases, ponies that are complete with all accessories will increase in price by $5 for ponies with only a brush and ribbon but can increase by $10 or greater depending on the number of accessories and their rarity (i.e. whether the accessory was available in only a single set or many sets).

Please note that the values presented in this guide are the average value that a particular pony will fetch in mint condition. The pony market is seasonal with higher prices around the holidays and lesser prices in the summer. The prices listed in this book are reflective of the public collecting market (such as auction sites, like eBay, or doll and collectible shows), however, prices can often be $5 less per pony or more when dealing collector to collector on My Little Pony message boards or fan sites. In addition, there are other factors that can contribute to a pony's value temporarily such as newsworthiness and mentions in pop culture (such as when the television show *The OC* featured Princess Sparkles of the Princess Ponies, temporarily increasing her value to $10 or more above her usual value).

# Understanding the Price Guide

Mint in box (MIB), mint on card (MOC) and never removed from box (NRFB) ponies are much harder to find and can vary greatly in value when they do appear. Depending on the rarity of the pony, being unopened can increase the value of the pony anywhere from $20 to $100 or greater than loose pony values.

# How to Identify a Real My Little Pony from a Fake

Not all My Little Ponies are in the typical pose or even the typical size and some are not even ponies at all but different animals. Often you may find yourself with something that looks like a My Little Pony at first glance that may actually not be a MLP at all. Many companies tried to cash in on the popularity of MLP with similar items that may look like MLP at first glance. Collector's usually refer to these imposters as fakies (pronounced fake-ies).

The simplest way to tell if what you have is a real MLP or not is to find the copyright. Usually on the hooves, if a pony item is marked by a company other than Hasbro, you are most likely not looking at a US issued MLP. Common knock-off companies are Ideal, Remco, Tara Toy Co, Buddy L Corp and American Greeting Card Co (Strawberry Shortcake dolls have some pony friends).

Now, if the item that you have says Hasbro, it may still not be a real MLP. Here is where this gets a little tricky. There are a few other items made by Hasbro that look like they might belong to the MLP set, but are actually part of totally different sets. The easiest of these to confuse are Cabbage Patch Ponies which are ponies (some are also unicorns or pegasus) slightly larger than MLP that are also maked Hasbro. However, they are also marked CPK (Cabbage Patch Kids) on their hooves and have the same chubby stitched look of the dolls. Other sets that are often confused with MLP are Moondreamers, Sweetie Pups and Fairy Tail Birds, all made by Hasbro.

**From left to right a CPK pony, Moondreamer, Fairy Tail Bird, and Sweetie Pup, all made by Hasbro but not MLP**

## Recurring Accessories

My Little Ponies were often accompanied with a multitude of accessories. From tiny toys to hair barrettes, from ribbons to princess wands, it can be daunting for a collector to keep track of all the tiny pieces. While some accessories were unique to an individual set, many were repeated throughout multiple sets. While unique accessories can be found on the individual pages of the set that they came with, to enable the largest photos of the ponies possible, all of the recurring accessories are pictured here for you to refer back to.

**Brushes and Combs**

Standard comb

Long standard comb

Crescent moon comb

Shooting star brush

Shooting star rainbow brush

Shooting star comb

Sun pick

Bird brush

Butterfly brush

Flower brush

Flower pick with colored centers

Flower pick

Glittery star pick

Solid star pick

Teddy bear brush

Duck comb

Recurring Accessories

Fish comb | Shell brush | Shell comb | Whale brush

Puppy brush | Racecar comb | Frog brush | Grasshopper comb

Kittens brush | Puppies comb | Bow/pony cameo comb | Wrapped candy comb

Oval grooming brush | Hearts and dots long brush | Hearts and dots long comb | Lollipop brush

**Hair ribbons** | **Barrettes**

Bird and lily barrette | Ice cream cone barrette | Sundae barrette

The My Little Pony G1 Collector's Inventory

| Lollipop barrette | Circle crown clip | Diamond crown clip | Oval crown clip |

| Flower barrette | Hearts barrette | "I Luv You" barrettes | Flower (lilies) barrette |

**Baby Accessories**

Shooting star barrette — Bassinet — Highchair

Playpen — Trimmed blankets — Rocker

Sandbox — Seesaw — Snail rocker

14

Recurring Accessories

Stroller

Wagon

Duck pull toy

Rattles (large and small)

Stacking toy

Xylophone and mallet

BABY necklace

Heart bib

Butterfly bib

Teddy bear bib

Neck bows

Newborn nightgown (white) and Newborn nightgown (pink)

White diaper and diaper box

Star panties

Bottle with trim

White and colored small bottles

Teeny Twin bottles

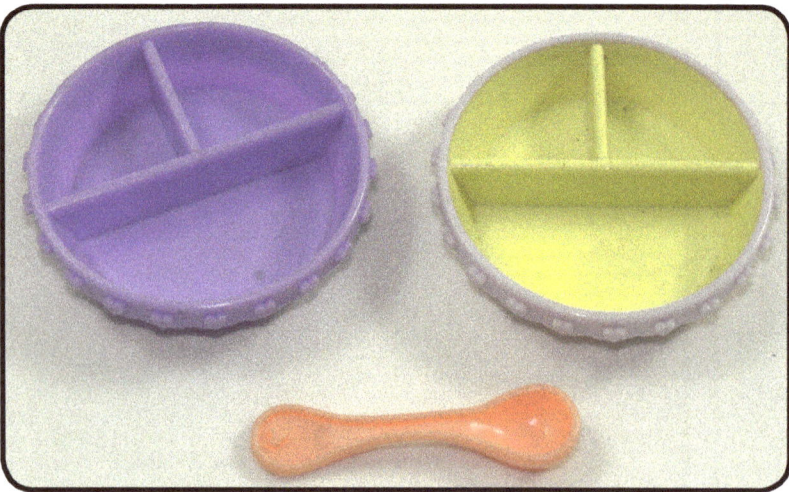

Dishes and spoon

# My Pretty Pony

Prior to the release of the Flat-Foot Collector Ponies set, in 1981 Hasbro offered a large plastic pony called My Pretty Pony under their Romper Room brand. The symbol for My Pretty Pony was the same as the rainbow that would later become the My Little Pony logo. A brown horse with a beige mane and tail, no symbol and a white star, her eye winked and ears wiggled when you "tickled" under her chin (by pulling a trigger-like switch). The brown version of My Pretty Pony was later released with a "baby" (Butterscotch of the Flat-Foot Collector Ponies) in a set called My Pretty Pony and Beautiful Baby. A version of the brown My Pretty Pony with a white spot on her side was also available, although it is unclear if she was sold individually or with the My Pretty Pony and Beautiful Baby set.

$10 to $15

❏ **My Pretty Pony** (with spot)
❏ **My Pretty Pony** (without spot)

$15 to $20

❏ Cowboy hat (white with red and white band)
❏ Blue ribbon
❏ Purple ribbon
❏ Red ribbon
❏ Powder blue long standard comb
❏ Powder blue grooming brush
❏ Red saddle blanket

The My Little Pony G1 Collector's Inventory

My Pretty Pony was later re-released with a peach colored body, pink hair and hearts on her rump painted just like the Pretty Parlor's Peachy, which is why My Pretty Pony is often considered the first My Little Pony.

$10 to $15

- ❏ **My Pretty Pony (Peachy)**
  - ❏ Cowboy hat (white with pink band)
  - ❏ Aqua ribbon
  - ❏ White ribbon
  - ❏ Yellow ribbon
  - ❏ Purple long standard comb
  - ❏ Purple grooming brush
  - ❏ Purple saddle blanket

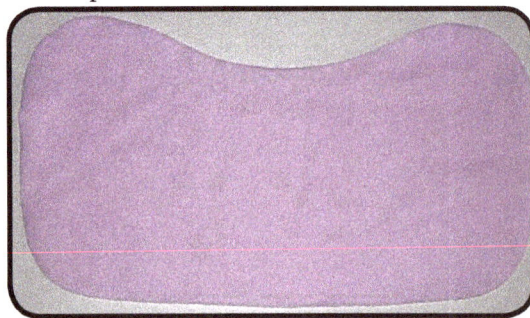

# 1982-1983
## Year 1

A set of six colorful ponies with unique symbols and brushable manes and tails, set the groundwork for what would become one of the most popular toy lines of all time.

# Original Ponies

During the first year of My Little Pony, Hasbro presented a set of 6 colorful ponies with brushable manes and tails. Each pony had a unique symbol on its rump, all four feet square and stood facing forward. Officially, this set was only named My Little Pony, but collectors refer to this set as the, Flat Foot Collector Ponies. This name originates from the unique hoof shape of this group. These ponies were later re-released with concave feet. Each pony came packaged on a bubble card with a brush and ribbon. The card included such phrases as: "She's a pretty, little, pony!" "My Little Pony is a pretty pony with long, shiny hair. She likes you to comb her hair so it stays silky and soft. You can braid her hair and tie a ribbon in it too!" and "Collect and play with all 6 little ponies. There's a pony in each of your favorite colors." The packaging included step-by-step instructions for braiding your pony's hair. The flat hooves are marked with the following information: Upper Left hoof: "copyright 1982 Hasbro", Upper right hoof: "Pat. Pending", Lower left hoof: "Made in", Lower right hoof: "Hong Kong."

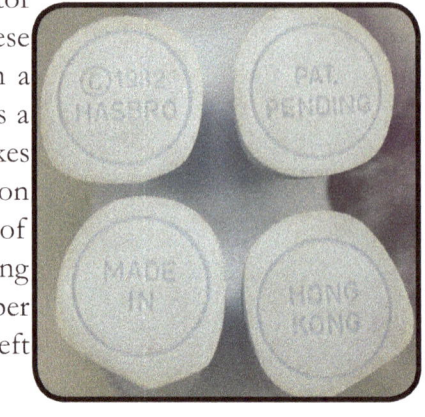

$5 to $10

❑ **Blossom**
❑ White standard comb
❑ White ribbon

❑ **Blue Belle**
❑ White standard comb
❑ White ribbon

$5 to $10

$5 to $10

❑ **Butterscotch**
❑ Pink standard comb
❑ Pink ribbon

❑ **Cotton Candy**
❑ Purple standard comb
❑ Light purple ribbon

$5 to $10

$10 to $15

❑ **Minty**
❑ Blue standard comb
❑ Light blue ribbon

❑ **Snuzzle**
❑ Blue standard comb
❑ White ribbon

$5 to $10

# 1983-1984
## Year 2

The second year of My Little Pony introduced some of the most beloved characters such as Applejack, Firefly, the Sea Ponies and others who were featured in the television special *Rescue at Midnight Castle*. This year also marked the entrance into the realm of magic as unicorns, pegasus and sea ponies joined the other ponies. The second year was also the first year for playsets and mail order offers.

The My Little Pony G1 Collector's Inventory

# Earth Ponies

While the first set of My Little Ponies had all been in the same pose (feet square, head down) this second set saw a variety of different poses. Blossom and Cotton Candy both returned from the first set of My Little Pony with a slight head lift and concave feet. This set also featured Seashell and Bubbles, the only two ponies ever released in the US in a seated position. In addition, Bow-Tie and Applejack had white freckles while Seashell and Bubbles had white stars on their faces. Both freckles and star markings were unique to this set. Each pony in this set came packaged on a bubble card with a flower brush, ribbon, and puffy sticker bearing their image.

$5 to $10

❏ **Applejack**
❏ Blue flower brush
❏ Blue ribbon
❏ Puffy sticker

❏ **Bow-Tie**
❏ Yellow flower brush
❏ Yellow ribbon
❏ Puffy sticker

$5 to $10

$10 to $15

❏ **Bubbles**
❏ Green flower brush
❏ Yellow ribbon
❏ Puffy sticker

❏ **Seashell**
❏ Dark pink flower brush
❏ Pink ribbon
❏ Puffy sticker

$10 to $15

$5 to $10

❏ **Blossom II**
❏ White flower brush
❏ White ribbon
❏ Puffy sticker

❏ **Cotton Candy II**
❏ Purple flower brush
❏ Light purple ribbon
❏ Puffy sticker

$5 to $10

1983-1984 Year 2

# Unicorn and Pegasus Ponies

Though all previous ponies had been regular ponies, My Little Pony entered the realm of magic with this set and never looked back. Each pony in this set not only was either a unicorn or pegasus but all had sparkly glittered symbols on their rump (rather than the painted acrylic ones of the past sets) and straight hair. Each Unicorn and Pegasus Pony came packaged on a bubble card with a shooting star brush, a ribbon, and a puffy sticker bearing their image. With the introduction of this set, MLP collectors coined the term earth pony to refer to a pony that was neither unicorn nor pegasus. **Collector's Note:** The glittery symbols are easily rubbed partially or completely off. This is an important factor to take into consideration when pricing a pony.

$5 to $10

- ❏ **Firefly**
  - ❏ Purple shooting star brush
  - ❏ Pink ribbon
  - ❏ Puffy sicker

$10 to $15

- ❏ **Glory**
  - ❏ Dark pink shooting star brush
  - ❏ Pink ribbon
  - ❏ Puffy sticker

$5 to $10

- ❏ **Medley**
  - ❏ Dark pink shooting star brush
  - ❏ Pink ribbon
  - ❏ Puffy sticker

$10 to $15

- ❏ **Moondancer**
  - ❏ Blue shooting star brush
  - ❏ White ribbon
  - ❏ Puffy sticker

$10 to $15

- ❏ **Sunbeam**
  - ❏ Yellow shooting star brush
  - ❏ Yellow ribbon
  - ❏ Puffy sticker

$10 to $15

- ❏ **Twilight**
  - ❏ Light blue shooting star brush
  - ❏ Light blue ribbon
  - ❏ Puffy sticker

*The My Little Pony G1 Collector's Inventory*

# Rainbow Ponies

The Rainbow Ponies marked the beginning of the mixed sets, i.e. sets that had unicorns, pegasus and earth ponies all together in one set. They had sparkly glittered symbols like the Unicorns and Pegasus set, but also had manes and tails that consisted of colors found in the My Little Pony rainbow logo: dark pink, yellow, green, and blue. Each Rainbow Pony came packaged with a shooting star brush with a rainbow sticker on it, a standard style comb, a ribbon, and a puffy sticker bearing their image. **Collector's Note:** These same six ponies were also released in 2008 in a special 25th anniversary set. Though the same molds as the ponies below, the 25th anniversary versions are considered part of the third generation of MLP because of their release date.

$5 to $10

- ❏ **Moonstone**
  - ❏ Purple rainbow brush
  - ❏ Purple standard comb
  - ❏ Pink ribbon
  - ❏ Puffy sticker

$5 to $10

- ❏ **Parasol**
  - ❏ Blue rainbow brush
  - ❏ Blue standard comb
  - ❏ Blue ribbon
  - ❏ Puffy sticker

$5 to $10

- ❏ **Skydancer**
  - ❏ Green rainbow brush
  - ❏ Green standard comb
  - ❏ Green ribbon
  - ❏ Puffy sticker

$5 to $10

- ❏ **Starshine**
  - ❏ Purple rainbow brush
  - ❏ Purple standard comb
  - ❏ Blue ribbon
  - ❏ Puffy sticker

$5 to $10

- ❏ **Sunlight**
  - ❏ Dark pink rainbow brush
  - ❏ Dark pink standard comb
  - ❏ Pink ribbon
  - ❏ Puffy sticker

$5 to $10

- ❏ **Windy**
  - ❏ Yellow rainbow brush
  - ❏ Yellow standard comb
  - ❏ Yellow ribbon
  - ❏ Puffy sticker

1983-1984 Year 2

# Sea Ponies

The Sea Ponies look like seahorses, with a curled tail and fins on the sides of their body, but their heads resembled a typical My Little Pony. Each Sea Pony contained a metal weight in the bottom of its tail to allow it to float upright when it was put in water. (**Collector's Note:** These weights often rust so many collectors choose to remove them.) Each Sea Pony also has a small round hole behind its ear to allow water to drain out. They are notorious for getting filled with mildew.

All Sea Ponies in this set came packaged with a clamshell stand that had a suction cup on the back so it could easily attach to your bathtub or bathroom tile, a shell brush, shell comb, and a ribbon. There are two versions of each of the Sea Ponies in this set, a version marked "patent pending" and a version that is not. Accessory colors may vary according to version. All Sea Ponies came packaged in a box with a plastic window front. Sea Ponies shell stands in mint condition are worth $10 to $15 each. Prices below are for loose mint condition Sea Ponies without accessories.

$5 to $10

❏ **Sealight**
    ❏ Pink shell brush (**Variation**: blue shell brush)
    ❏ Pink shell comb (**Variation**: blue shell comb)
    ❏ Green clamshell
    ❏ Yellow ribbon

$5 to $10

❏ **Seawinkle**
    ❏ Blue shell brush
    ❏ Blue shell comb
    ❏ Pink clamshell
    ❏ Yellow ribbon

$5 to $10

❏ **Wavedancer**
    ❏ Blue shell brush (**Variation**: pink shell brush)
    ❏ Blue shell comb (**Variation**: pink shell comb)
    ❏ Purple clamshell
    ❏ Purple ribbon

# 1984-1985
## Year 3

The ponies released in the third year were some of the better known as they were all featured in the animated television special *Escape from Catrina*. The introduction of Baby Ponies was a triumph of the third year of My Little Pony, with babies, the nursery and Pony Wear all given prominence in the television special. In addition to more Unicorns, Pegasus, Sea Ponies, and Rainbow Ponies, the Baby Sea Ponies found a place in the My Little Pony family and would eventually replace their adult counterparts. The popular human character of Megan and her pony friend Sundance also debuted this year.

The My Little Pony G1 Collector's Inventory

# Earth Ponies
**(second set)**

In the third year of MLP, there was a new batch of earth ponies and Applejack and Bow Tie returned with longer, curly manes. Each came with a brush, ribbon and puffy sticker in their image. **Collector's Note**: Lickety Split and Posey had pink hair that was very prone to fading in direct sunlight. Faded hair may appear white. It is good idea to keep your ponies with "Posey Pink" hair out of the sun as well as to take faded hair into consideration when pricing. Posey and Tootsie's symbols can also fade to white.

$5 to $10

❏ **Applejack II**
❏ Neon pink butterfly brush
❏ Yellow ribbon
❏ Puffy sticker

❏ **Bow-Tie II**
❏ Purple butterfly brush
❏ White ribbon
❏ Puffy sticker

$5 to $10

$5 to $10

❏ **Cherries Jubilee**
❏ Green butterfly brush
❏ Green ribbon
❏ Puffy sticker

❏ **Lickety-Split**
❏ Purple butterfly brush
❏ White ribbon
❏ Puffy sticker

$5 to $10

$5 to $10

❏ **Posey**
❏ Blue butterfly brush
❏ Yellow ribbon
❏ Puffy sticker

❏ **Tootsie**
❏ Coral butterfly brush
❏ Yellow ribbon
❏ Puffy sticker

$5 to $10

1984-1985 Year 3

# Unicorns and Pegasus
### (second set)

The Unicorn and Pegasus set returned with new friends and each pony still had a glittery symbol. A few of the ponies from last year's set returned. Both Medley and Firefly had curly hair in this issue while Moondancer and Glory were identical to the previous issue. Each came on a bubble card with a moon comb, ribbon, and puffy sticker in their image.

$5 to $10

❏ **Firefly II**
❏ Yellow crescent moon comb
❏ Pink ribbon
❏ Puffy sticker

$5 to $10

❏ **Medley II**
❏ Pink crescent moon comb
❏ White ribbon
❏ Puffy sticker

$10 to $15

❏ **Heart Throb**
❏ Lime-green crescent moon comb
❏ Light blue ribbon
❏ Puffy sticker

$10 to $15

❏ **Gusty**
❏ Pink crescent moon comb
❏ Pink ribbon
❏ Puffy sticker

$10 to $15

❏ **Powder**
❏ Aqua crescent moon comb
❏ Bright pink ribbon
❏ Puffy sticker

$10 to $15

❏ **Skyflier**
❏ Purple crescent moon comb
❏ Aqua blue ribbon
❏ Puffy sticker

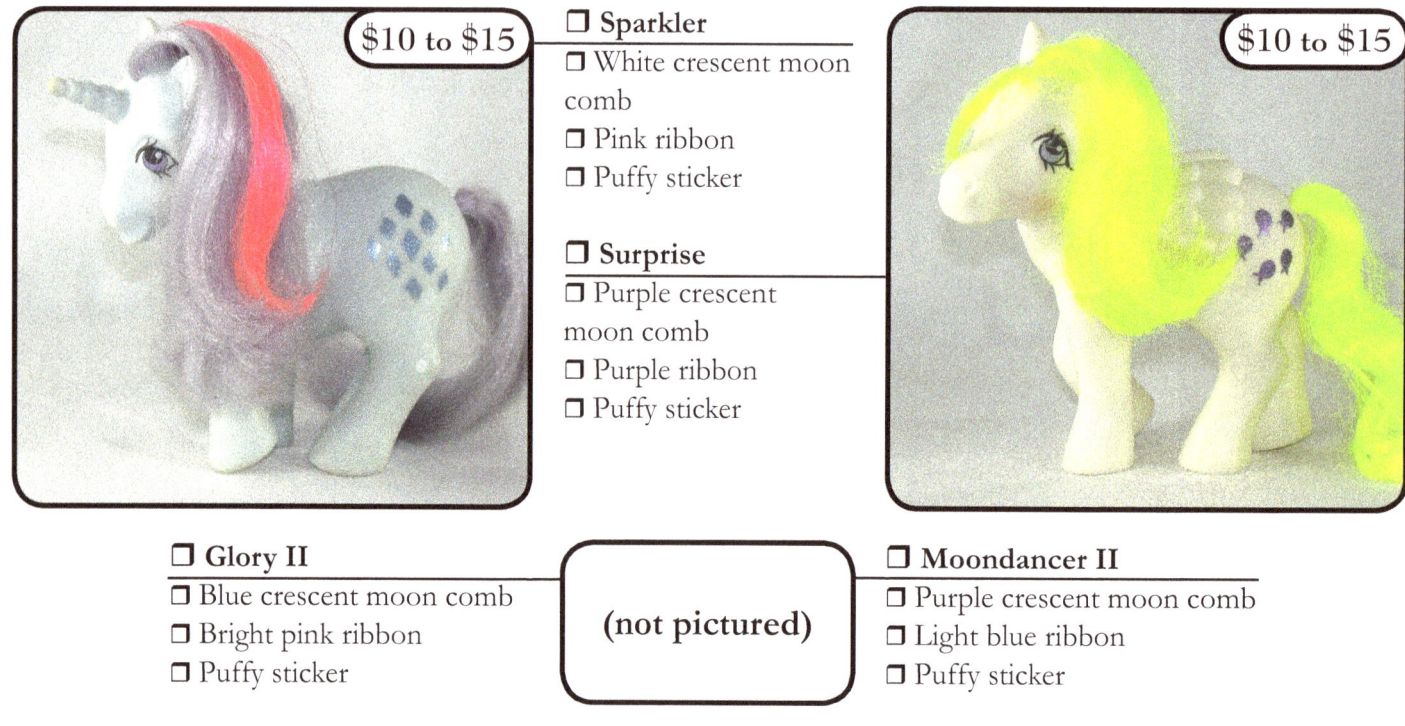

- ☐ **Sparkler**
  - ☐ White crescent moon comb
  - ☐ Pink ribbon
  - ☐ Puffy sticker
- ☐ **Surprise**
  - ☐ Purple crescent moon comb
  - ☐ Purple ribbon
  - ☐ Puffy sticker
- ☐ **Glory II**
  - ☐ Blue crescent moon comb
  - ☐ Bright pink ribbon
  - ☐ Puffy sticker
- ☐ **Moondancer II**
  - ☐ Purple crescent moon comb
  - ☐ Light blue ribbon
  - ☐ Puffy sticker

$10 to $15 (Sparkler, Surprise)
(not pictured) — Glory II, Moondancer II

# Megan and Sundance

Megan, the human friend of the ponies and star of the first two animated specials, was featured in this set with Sundance, the star of *Escape from Catrina*. Megan came dressed in a white dress with pink trim, white panties, pink shoes, and a pink hair ribbon. Sundance came with a pink bridle with a white flower and an aqua blue tail ribbon. The set came packaged in a box with a blue flower brush, a blue comb and a puffy sticker. **Collector's Note**: There are two other versions of Megan and Sundance that were sold in the United States: So-Soft Megan and Sundance and Twice as Fancy Megan and Sundance. Megan and Sundance were always sold together in stores. They were also available as a set through the mail order program. Complete with all accessories, this set increases $10 or more in value.

- ☐ **Megan**
- ☐ **Sundance**
  - ☐ White dress with pink trim
  - ☐ White panties
  - ☐ 2 pink shoes (for Megan)
  - ☐ Pink ribbon
  - ☐ Aqua blue ribbon
  - ☐ Pink bridle with white flower
  - ☐ Blue flower brush
  - ☐ Blue standard comb
  - ☐ Puffy sticker

$5 to $10

1984-1985 Year 3

# Rainbow Ponies
**(second set)**

The second set of Rainbow Ponies' hair, instead of the richer colors of the last set, was composed of the following colors: melon, pink, blue, and chartreuse. Each came with a brush, ribbon and puffy sticker in their image. **Collector's Note:** This set of Rainbow Ponies is less common than the first set and thus more valuable to collectors. Their glittery metallic symbols are prone to rusting as well as symbol damage. This is an important factor to keep in mind when pricing ponies in this set. This set of Rainbow Ponies were later re-released as a mail order with slightly darker glitter symbols.

$10 to $15

❑ **Confetti**
❑ Blue rainbow brush
❑ Blue standard comb
❑ Pink ribbon
❑ Puffy sticker

$10 to $15

❑ **Flutterbye**
❑ Aqua rainbow brush
❑ Aqua standard comb
❑ Yellow ribbon
❑ Puffy sticker

$10 to $15

❑ **Pinwheel**
❑ Purple rainbow brush
❑ Purple standard comb
❑ Purple ribbon
❑ Puffy sticker

$10 to $15

❑ **Starflower**
❑ Pink rainbow brush
❑ Pink standard comb
❑ Purple ribbon
❑ Puffy sticker

$10 to $15

❑ **Tickle**
❑ Lime rainbow brush
❑ Lime standard comb
❑ Turquoise ribbon
❑ Puffy sticker

$10 to $15

❑ **Trickles**
❑ Light pink rainbow brush
❑ Light pink comb
❑ Bright yellow ribbon
❑ Puffy sticker

# Baby Ponies

The Baby Ponies were the first complete set of babies offered in stores. The only baby pony available pervious to this set was a mail order version of Baby Ember that did not have a symbol as the ponies of this set did. This set of Baby Ponies were the children of ponies from the original sets of unicorn, pegasus and earth ponies. In some cases, their hair color was a softer hue than that of their mother. Each Baby Pony was packaged in a box with a variety of accessories including cloth diapers in cardboard boxes, playpens (which can come apart and flatten), and ID bracelet style necklaces that spell out BABY. Prices listed are for loose ponies and can increase $10 or more for ponies with accessories. **Collector's Note:** Pearly versions of these baby ponies were also available through the horseshoe points mail order program several years later.

**❏ Baby Blossom**
   ❏ Pink bear brush
   ❏ Diaper and box
   ❏ White bottle with aqua trim
   ❏ Pink with white top rattle
   ❏ Pink elastic
   ❏ Aqua rocker
   ❏ Heart bib with blue trim
   ❏ Pink BABY necklace
   ❏ Light pink ribbon
   ❏ Puffy sticker

**❏ Baby Cotton Candy**
   ❏ Lavender bear brush
   ❏ Diaper and box
   ❏ White bottle with yellow trim
   ❏ Duck pull toy
   ❏ Purple playpen
   ❏ Pink and white heart blanket
   ❏ Pink BABY necklace
   ❏ Purple ribbon
   ❏ Puffy sticker

**❏ Baby Firefly**
   ❏ Lavender bear brush
   ❏ Diaper with box
   ❏ White bottle with pink (or blue) trim
   ❏ Blue with white top rattle
   ❏ White playpen
   ❏ Blue and white heart blanket
   ❏ White BABY necklace
   ❏ Purple ribbon
   ❏ Puffy sticker

1984-1985 Year 3

❏ **Baby Glory**
　❏ Dark pink bear brush
　❏ Diaper and box
　❏ White bottle with blue trim
　❏ Stack toy
　❏ Pink playpen
　❏ Purple and white star blanket
　❏ Pink BABY necklace
　❏ Pink ribbon
　❏ Puffy sticker

$5 to $10

❏ **Baby Moondancer**
　❏ Blue bear brush
　❏ Diaper with box
　❏ White bottle with lavender trim
　❏ Duck pull toy
　❏ Purple rocker
　❏ Heart bib with purple trim
　❏ Pink BABY necklace
　❏ Blue ribbon
　❏ Puffy sticker

$5 to $10

❏ **Baby Surprise**
　❏ Yellow bear brush
　❏ Diaper with box
　❏ White bottle with green trim
　❏ Stack toy
　❏ Pink rocker
　❏ Heart bib with pink trim
　❏ White BABY necklace
　❏ Pink ribbon
　❏ Puffy sticker

$5 to $10

The My Little Pony G1 Collector's Inventory

# Sea Ponies

### (second set)

The Sea Ponies returned in full force this year, with shell stands in both clamshell and a new conch shell shape. Some newcomers also had a stripe of a different color in their manes, unlike the set from the previous year, which had only solid color manes. In addition to a shell stand, all Sea Ponies were boxed with a shell brush, a shell comb, a ribbon, and a puffy sticker. This was the last set of adult Sea Ponies ever made. From this point forward, there were only Baby Sea Ponies.

The prices listed below are for loose, mint condition ponies of this set. Sea Ponies of this set with their shell stands are valued at $90 or greater.

$40 & up

### ❏ High Tide
❏ Light pink shell brush
❏ Light pink shell comb
❏ Lavender clamshell
❏ Purple ribbon
❏ Puffy sticker

### ❏ Sand Dollar
❏ Purple shell brush
❏ Purple shell comb
❏ Aqua clamshell
❏ Pink ribbon
❏ Puffy sticker

$40 & up

$40 & up

### ❏ Sea Breeze
❏ Blue shell brush
❏ Blue shell comb
❏ Mint-green swirl shell
❏ Pink ribbon
❏ Puffy sticker

### ❏ Sea Mist
❏ Dark purple shell brush
❏ Dark purple shell comb
❏ Darker pink-purple swirl shell
❏ Pink ribbon
❏ Puffy sticker

$40 & up

1984–1985 Year 3

❏ **Wave Jumper**
❏ Pink shell brush
❏ Pink shell comb
❏ Green clamshell
❏ Yellow ribbon
❏ Puffy sticker

❏ **Whitecap**
❏ Dark purple shell brush
❏ Dark purple shell comb
❏ Pink swirl shell
❏ White ribbon (**Variation**: turquoise)
❏ Puffy sticker

$40 & up

$40 & up

## Baby Sea Ponies

Baby Sea Ponies found their way into many collector's hearts…and bathtubs! The Baby Sea Ponies were first introduced in year three, but many other sets were released in later years. Baby Sea Ponies had brushable manes and did not have the metal weights that caused rust issues in the adults. Each Baby Sea Pony in this set had a forelock and came packaged with a whale brush and its own special float in the shape of a fish, duck, or turtle. Each Baby Sea Pony had a hole behind one ear to allow water to drain out.

Baby Sea Pony floats from this set are valued at $5 to $10 by themselves. Prices below are for pony only. **Collector's Note**: Surf Rider's pink hair can fade easily to white.

$5 to $10

❏ **Backstroke**
❏ Aqua and orange fish float
❏ Dark pink whale brush
❏ Yellow ribbon
❏ Puffy sticker

❏ **Sea Shimmer**
❏ Purple and green turtle float
❏ Blue whale brush
❏ Pink ribbon
❏ Puffy sticker

$5 to $10

The My Little Pony G1 Collector's Inventory

$5 to $10

- **Sea Star**
  - Pink and purple duck float
  - Pink whale brush
  - Pink ribbon
  - Puffy sticker

- **Splasher**
  - Green and blue turtle float
  - Lavender whale brush
  - Pink ribbon
  - Puffy sticker

$5 to $10

$5 to $10

- **Surf Rider**
  - Blue and purple fish float
  - Pink-lavender whale brush
  - Light aqua ribbon
  - Puffy sticker

- **Tiny Bubbles**
  - Yellow and orange duck float
  - Blue whale brush
  - Orange ribbon
  - Puffy sticker

$5 to $10

## "Ember's Dream"

Released as part of the *Listen 'n Fun* series from Hasbro, this set contained a pony and a cassette tape entitled, *Ember's Dream*. Though Ember was the name of the original mail order baby pony, this version of Ember from the *Ember's Dream* pack had a white star as her symbol. There is a hard to find variation of this item where the name of the story is printed on the packaging as *Amber's Dream*.

- Ember
  - *Ember's Dream* cassette tape

$10 to $15

$5 to $10

# 1985-1986
## Year 4

*My Little Pony: The Movie* was released in movie theatres during this year so pony fans saw more new pony characters and other items than ever before. Megan and Sundance changed their appearance and Megan's little sister, Molly, joined the fun with her own pony friend, Baby Sundance. The Flutter Ponies set became wildly popular (despite their infamously fragile wings), Baby Ponies with Beddy Bye Eyes opened and closed their eyes for sleep and new flocked So Soft Ponies and Twinkle Eyed Ponies captivated the imagination. As the stars of the movie later went on to star in the *My Little Pony* syndicated cartoon series, the ponies of this year are also fan favorites and some of the best known.

# So-Soft Ponies

"A beautiful pony that's soft and furry all over." So-Soft Ponies were ponies whose bodies were covered with soft flocking making them fuzzy. This flocking had a tendency to rub off in the following areas especially: hooves, muzzle, horn, and ear tips. Three of these So Soft Ponies were created in a unique rearing pose and came packaged with clear plastic stands. Several of the ponies in this set had previously been released in non-so-soft form in the year prior. All So Soft Ponies were sold on a bubble card with a brush or comb, and a ribbon.

$10 to $15

- **Bouncy**
  - Dark orange sun pick
  - Scented body sticker
  - Dark pink ribbon

- **Buttons**
  - Yellow sun pick
  - Scented body sticker
  - Pink ribbon

$10 to $15

- **Cherries Jubilee**
  - Green butterfly brush (**Variation**: dark pink butterfly brush)
  - Scented body sticker
  - Yellow ribbon

- **Cupcake**
  - Orange sun pick
  - Scented body sticker
  - Pinkish purple ribbon

$10 to $15

$10 to $15

- **Fifi**
  - Purple sun pick
  - Scented body sticker
  - Blue ribbon

- **Gusty**
  - Pink crescent moon comb (**Variation**: pink shooting star comb)
  - Scented body sticker
  - Pink ribbon

$10 to $15

$10 to $15

1985-1986 Year 4

$10 to $15

- **Heart Throb**
  - Light green crescent moon comb
  - Scented body sticker
  - Light blue ribbon

$10 to $15

- **Hippity-Hop**
  - Purple bird brush
  - Scented body sticker
  - White ribbon

$10 to $15

- **Lickety-Split**
  - Purple butterfly brush
  - Scented body sticker
  - White ribbon

$10 to $15

- **Lofty**
  - Blue sun pick
  - Scented body sticker
  - Blue ribbon

$10 to $15

- **Magic Star**
  - Bright pink bird brush (**Variation**: orange)
  - Scented body sticker
  - Bright pink ribbon
  - Clear stand (fit into holes in her feet)

$10 to $15

- **North Star**
  - Dark pink bird brush
  - Scented body sticker
  - Blue ribbon

$10 to $15

- **Paradise**
  - Green sun pick
  - Scented body sticker
  - Green ribbon

- **Posey**
  - Aqua butterfly brush
  - Scented body sticker
  - Green ribbon

$10 to $15

39

The My Little Pony G1 Collector's Inventory

$10 to $15

- **Ribbon**
  - Dark pink bird brush
  - Scented body sticker
  - Bright orange ribbon

- **Scrumptious**
  - Light green sun pick
  - Scented body sticker
  - Yellow ribbon

$10 to $15

$10 to $15

- **Shady**
  - Dark purple sun pick
  - Scented body sticker
  - Blue ribbon

- **Skippity-Doo**
  - Pink sun pick
  - Scented body sticker
  - Pink ribbon
  - Clear stand (fits into holes in her feet)

$10 to $15

$10 to $15

- **Surprise**
  - Purple crescent moon comb
  - Scented body sticker
  - Purple ribbon

- **Truly**
  - Dark aqua sun pick
  - Scented body sticker
  - Aqua ribbon
  - Clear stand (fits into holes in her feet)

$10 to $15

- **Twist**
  - Yellow bird brush
  - Scented body sticker
  - Lavender ribbon

- **Wind Whistler**
  - Purple bird brush
  - Scented body sticker
  - White ribbon

$10 to $15

1985-1986 Year 4

# Baby Pony with Beddy Bye Eyes

These Baby Ponies, like the first set, were the children of the unicorn, pegasus, and earth pony sets of the past. They featured special eyes with eyelashes that that closed when you laid the pony on its side to sleep and opened again when you placed the pony upright. Beddy Bye Eyes Ponies were slightly smaller than regular baby ponies. They were packaged in a box with a many accessories. **Collector's Note:** Beddy Bye Eyed ponies can rust very easily around the eyes and eyelashes can come out from wear. Make sure to adjust value accordingly if your pony is either rusted or missing eyelashes. If a pony from this set is complete with all accessories, their value can increase by $10 or more.

$5 to $10

- ❑ **Baby Gusty**
    - ❑ Purple duck comb
    - ❑ Scented body sticker
    - ❑ Pinkish purple ribbon
    - ❑ Purple high chair with yellow tray
    - ❑ Blue with white text BABY necklace
    - ❑ Pinkish purple trimmed heart bib
    - ❑ Duck toy
    - ❑ Yellow trimmed bottle
    - ❑ White diaper
    - ❑ Diaper box

- ❑ **Baby Heart Throb**
    - ❑ Light purple duck comb
    - ❑ Scented body sticker
    - ❑ Light blue ribbon
    - ❑ Yellow playpen
    - ❑ White with peach text BABY necklace
    - ❑ Light pink trimmed heart blanket
    - ❑ Pink dish with yellow inside
    - ❑ Aqua spoon
    - ❑ Light blue trimmed bottle
    - ❑ White diaper
    - ❑ Diaper box

$5 to $10

$5 to $10

- ❑ **Baby Lickety-Split**
    - ❑ Aqua duck comb
    - ❑ Scented body sticker
    - ❑ White ribbon
    - ❑ Yellow high chair with pink tray
    - ❑ White with peach text BABY necklace
    - ❑ Aqua blue trimmed heart bib
    - ❑ Pink trimmed bottle
    - ❑ Aqua dish with white inside
    - ❑ Light yellow spoon
    - ❑ White diaper
    - ❑ Diaper box

- **Baby Lofty**
    - Pink duck comb
    - Scented body sticker
    - Pink ribbon
    - Blue and yellow wagon with white axles
    - Purple-pink with white text BABY necklace
    - Duck pull toy
    - Pastel xylophone
    - Aqua mallet
    - Pink trimmed bottle
    - White diaper
    - Diaper box

$5 to $10

$5 to $10

- **Baby Ribbon**
    - Aqua duck comb
    - Scented body sticker
    - White ribbon
    - Pink and aqua wagon
    - Purple-pink with white text BABY necklace
    - Pastel xylophone
    - Aqua mallet
    - Duck toy
    - Aqua trimmed bottle
    - White diaper
    - Diaper box

- **Baby Shady**
    - Blue duck comb (**Variation**: green duck comb)
    - Scented body sticker
    - Pink ribbon
    - Light pink playpen
    - Aqua with white text BABY necklace
    - Purple trimmed stars blanket
    - Aqua-green trimmed heart bib
    - Duck toy
    - Yellow trimmed bottle
    - White diaper
    - Diaper box

$5 to $10

1985-1986 Year 4

# Twinkle Eyed

"Her eyes sparkle and shine like precious jewels." Twinkle Eyed Ponies, often abbreviated to just TE by collectors, had sparkly jewels for eyes and multicolor hair. Each pony was packaged on a bubble card with a shooting star comb, ribbon and scented body sticker.

$5 to $10

- ❏ **Fizzy**
  - ❏ Purple-pink shooting stars comb
  - ❏ Scented body sticker
  - ❏ Pink ribbon

$5 to $10

- ❏ **Galaxy**
  - ❏ Blue shooting stars comb
  - ❏ Scented body sticker
  - ❏ Powder blue ribbon

- ❏ **Gingerbread**
  - ❏ Blue shooting stars comb
  - ❏ Scented body sticker
  - ❏ Pinkish-purple ribbon

$5 to $10

$5 to $10

- ❏ **Masquerade**
  - ❏ Pink shooting stars comb
  - ❏ Scented body sticker
  - ❏ Pink ribbon

- ❏ **Sky Rocket**
  - ❏ Pink shooting stars comb
  - ❏ Scented body sticker
  - ❏ Purple ribbon

$5 to $10

$5 to $10

- ❏ **Speedy**
  - ❏ Yellow shooting stars comb
  - ❏ Scented body sticker
  - ❏ Blue ribbon

- ❏ **Sweet Pop**
  - ❏ Purple shooting stars comb
  - ❏ Scented body sticker
  - ❏ Pink ribbon

$5 to $10

43

- **Sweet Stuff**
  - Yellow shooting stars comb
  - Scented body sticker
  - Yellow ribbon

- **Whizzer**
  - Purple shooting stars comb
  - Scented body sticker
  - White ribbon

## Megan & So-Soft Sundance

This year, Megan and Sundance returned. While Megan was nearly the same as her original release (her eyelashes were thinner and her eyebrows were darker in this release), Sundance was now sporting the latest fashion trend: So-Soft flocking. Aside from the flocking, she was the exact same pony as the original release. The set came packaged in a box with a purple bird brush, purple original comb, and a body sticker. This set with all accessories is valued at $20 to $30.

- **Megan**
- **Sundance** (So-Soft)
  - White dress with pink hearts and flowers
  - Lavender shoes (w/molded hearts)
  - White panties
  - Dark pink hair ribbon
- Dark pink bridle with a white flower on the crown piece with reins
- Purple bird brush
- Purple standard comb
- Body sticker of Megan and Sundance

1985-1986 Year 4

# Flutter Ponies

"A gentle touch lets her beautiful wings flutter up and down." The Flutter Ponies, who saved Dream Valley from the Smooze in *My Little Pony: The Movie*, were smaller and thinner than the average pony. They had a small marking on either their cheek or forehead that matched their symbol. Flutter Ponies had iridescent wings that were attached to a mechanism that allowed the wings to flap when you pressed the shell shaped button between the wings. Sadly, the wings were very fragile and it is very rare to find a Flutter Pony whose original wings are attached and intact. Some collectors have created (and many privately sell) replacement wings that you can use for display in place of the original Hasbro made wings. Some Flutter Ponies have alternant head molds that are larger and have bigger eyes. Despite these differences, neither mold seems to be more common. Flutter Ponies were sold with a metallic ribbon and a dual colored flower pick. They were packaged in a box with a plastic window. Prices below are for mint condition Flutter Ponies with wings. Without wings, Flutter Ponies are valued at only $1 to $5.

$35 to $40

❑ **Forget-Me-Not**
- ❑ Pink/ purple flower pick
- ❑ Silver metallic ribbon
- ❑ Scented body sticker
- ❑ 2 wings

❑ **Honeysuckle**
- ❑ Blue/yellow flower pick
- ❑ Gold metallic ribbon
- ❑ Scented body sticker
- ❑ 2 wings

$35 to $40

$35 to $40

❑ **Lily**
- ❑ Blue/green lower pick
- ❑ Silver metallic ribbon
- ❑ Scented body sticker
- ❑ 2 wings

❑ **Morning Glory**
- ❑ Pink/green flower pick
- ❑ Gold metallic ribbon
- ❑ Scented body sticker
- ❑ 2 wings

$35 to $40

$35 to $40

❑ **Peach Blossom**
- ❑ Purple/pink flower pick
- ❑ Silver metallic ribbon
- ❑ Scented body sticker
- ❑ 2 wings

❑ **Rosedust**
- ❑ Green/pink flower pick
- ❑ Gold metallic ribbon
- ❑ Scented body sticker
- ❑ 2 wings

$35 to $40

The My Little Pony G1 Collector's Inventory

# Pretty 'N Pearly Baby Sea Ponies

"With shimmery bodies." This fancier set of Baby Sea Ponies came with a pearly glaze all over their bodies. They also had floats like their predecessors, but their floats came in different animal shapes. Surf Rider and Sea Shimmer returned in this set with pearly bodies. Each Pretty 'n Pearly Baby Sea Pony came packaged on a bubble card with a float, a whale brush or fish comb, and a flat scented body sticker. Floats are valued at $5 to $10 by themselves.

$5 to $10

- ❏ **Beachcomber**
    - ❏ Pink/green alligator float
    - ❏ Light purple fish shaped comb
    - ❏ Pink ribbon
    - ❏ Scented body sticker

- ❏ **Ripple**
    - ❏ Green/pink frog float
    - ❏ Mint green fish shaped comb
    - ❏ White ribbon
    - ❏ Scented body sticker

$5 to $10

$5 to $10

- ❏ **Sea Shimmer**
    - ❏ Purple/green turtle float
    - ❏ Light purple whale shaped brush
    - ❏ Pink ribbon
    - ❏ Scented body sticker

- ❏ **Sunshower**
    - ❏ Blue/yellow alligator float
    - ❏ Yellow fish shaped comb
    - ❏ White ribbon
    - ❏ Scented body sticker

$5 to $10

$5 to $10

- ❏ **Surf Rider**
    - ❏ Blue/purple fish float
    - ❏ Pink whale shaped brush
    - ❏ Blue ribbon
    - ❏ Scented body sticker

- ❏ **Water Lily**
    - ❏ Purple/green frog float
    - ❏ Light blue fish shaped comb
    - ❏ Blue ribbon
    - ❏ Scented body sticker

$5 to $10

1985-1986 Year 4

# Party Gift Pack

"5 special ponies and over 50 accessories help you celebrate!" Sold as a boxed gift set, the Party Pack was a sampler of every new type of pony released in the last year. It featured a So-Soft, a Twinkle Eyed, a Baby Pony with Beddy Bye Eyes a Flutter Pony and a Pretty 'n Pearly Baby Sea Pony. The set also came with a large number of accessories for the ponies to party with.

Accessories from this set are hard to find and highly sought after. The accessories can be worth $25 or more even without the ponies. The price listed below is for Yum Yum in mint condition with wings. Without, she is only worth $5 to $10.

$5 to $10

❑ **Celebrate** (Pretty 'n Pearly Baby Sea Pony)
   ❑ Celebrate's purple/orange turtle float

$5 to $10

❑ **Baby Frosting** (Beddy Bye Eyes)

$5 to $10

❑ **Best Wishes** (So-Soft)

$5 to $10

❑ **Party Time** (Twinkle Eyed)

$35 to $40

❑ **Yum Yum** (Flutter Pony)

- 5 party hats
  - blue & orange balloon design w/pink pompom
  - yellow & aqua diamond design w/aqua pompom
  - aqua & pink flower design w/yellow pompom
  - pink & green wave design w/white pompom
  - yellow & dark pink fish design w/light blue pompom
- 1 birthday cake (white with yellow trim)
- Pink candles (removable)
- 1 blue cake serving plate
- 6 (yellow) cups
- 6 (blue) plates
- 5 party favors
  - pink
  - orange
  - green
  - blue
  - purple
- Pin-the-Tail on the Pony game
- 1 orange blindfold
- 1 purple blindfold
- 2 pink tails (for game)
- "It's a Party" blanket
- "It's Party Time" sign
- Party diaper (white w/colored stars)
- Diaper box (with picture of Baby Frosting)
- Balloon (light green w/pink stick)
- Decorated gift box

- 5 pony-sized invitations (that pictures Yum Yum)
- 1 postcard (that pictures Best Wishes)
- Pale pink flower brush
- 4 ribbons (green, orange, silver, purple-pink)
- Yellow sun pick
- Body sticker

48

1985-1986 Year 4

# Molly & Baby Sundance

While big sister Megan was teaching Sundance how to stick those landings in *Escape from Catrina*, Molly had made a friend of her own. Like Sundance and big sister, Molly and Baby Sundance (with Beddy Bye Eyes) came with a bridle and dress for Molly. Unlike Megan, however, no new outfits were ever released for Molly. The set was packaged in a box with a bird brush, standard comb, and ribbon.

❏ **Molly**
❏ **Baby Sundance**

    ❏ 2 pink ponytail ribbons
    ❏ Pink dress w/white dots and pink/white trim
    ❏ Rainbow tights
    ❏ White shoes
    ❏ Pink velvet bridle with a white flower in the center of the crown piece with reins
    ❏ Hair ribbon
    ❏ Pink bird brush
    ❏ Pink standard comb
    ❏ Body sticker featuring Molly and Baby Sundance

$5 to $10

$10 to $15

# 1986-1987
## Year 5

Princess Ponies, Big Brother Ponies, Newborn Ponies, First Tooth Ponies and Twice As Fancy Ponies (to name a few) joined new sets of So Soft and Twinkle Eyed Ponies in Year 5. Many of the characters released this year were also part of the animated My Little Pony television series and these television stars are better known and more sought after, then their lesser known counterparts.

# Baby Ponies with First Tooth

The First Tooth Baby Ponies were the children of both So-Soft and Twinkle Eyed mothers (though the babies were not So-Soft or Twinkle Eyed themselves). Each pony had a single tooth and came with lots of accessories having to do with teething and dental hygiene, many of which were unique to this set (pictured below). Some ponies in this set also came with a mini-Gloworm (another popular Hasbro toy whose cartoon was often back to back with the MLP series). Baby Lickety Split, star of *My Little Pony: The Movie* and formerly of the Beddy Bye Eyes set, was reissued this year with a First Tooth. Oddly enough, though adult Fifi from the So-Soft set was a unicorn, First Tooth Baby Fifi is an earth pony. Each pony came packaged in a box. Accessories from this set are hard to find and can run $10 or more for the accessories even with out the pony.

$5 to $10

$5 to $10

- **Baby Bouncy**
    - Pink toothpaste
    - Blue toothbrush
    - White sippy cup
    - Pastel xylophone
    - Aqua mallet
    - Star panties
    - Yellow duck comb
    - Dark pink ribbon

- **Baby Fifi**
    - Peach toothpaste
    - Blue toothbrush
    - White sippy cup
    - Pastel xylophone
    - Aqua mallet
    - Star panties
    - Purple duck comb
    - Pink ribbon

1986-1987 Year 5

$5 to $10

❑ **Baby Northstar**
  ❑ Aqua toothpaste
  ❑ Purple toothbrush
  ❑ Aqua teething ring
  ❑ Gloworm
  ❑ Star panties
  ❑ Pink duck comb
  ❑ Blue ribbon

$5 to $10

❑ **Baby Lickety-Split**
  ❑ Yellow toothpaste
  ❑ Aqua toothbrush
  ❑ Pink teething ring
  ❑ Gloworm
  ❑ Star panties
  ❑ Aqua duck comb
  ❑ White ribbon

$5 to $10

❑ **Baby Quackers**
  ❑ Blue toothpaste
  ❑ Pink toothbrush
  ❑ First tooth pillow
  ❑ Felt tooth
  ❑ Stack toy
  ❑ Star panties
  ❑ Purple duck comb
  ❑ Orange ribbon

$5 to $10

❑ **Baby Tic Tac Toe**
  ❑ Green toothpaste
  ❑ Aqua toothbrush
  ❑ First tooth pillow
  ❑ Felt tooth
  ❑ Stack toy
  ❑ Star panties
  ❑ Pink duck comb
  ❑ White ribbon

# Big Brother Ponies

After years of waiting, the first male ponies joined My Little Pony this year. Called the Big Brother Ponies, they were larger than female ponies and had Clydesdale-type furry hooves. Like the Village People of Dream Valley, Big Brother Ponies came dressed in various hats and colorful bandanas to match their symbols. Each Big Brother Pony was sold on a bubble card with a hat, bandana, and either a grasshopper comb or frog brush. Big Brother hats and bandanas are sought after and can fetch $15 or more by themselves. Ponies in this set with all accessories more than double in value.

$15 to $20

- **4-Speed**
  - Purple frog brush
  - Yellow hard hat
  - Purple bandana

$15 to $20

- **Quarterback**
  - Pink grasshopper comb
  - Pink football helmet
  - Pink bandana

$15 to $20

- **Salty**
  - Yellow frog brush
  - White sailor's hat
  - Green bandana

$15 to $20

- **Slugger**
  - Blue grasshopper comb
  - Blue baseball cap
  - Light blue bandana

$15 to $20

- **Steamer**
  - Mint green frog brush
  - Purple engineer's hat
  - Light yellow bandana

$15 to $20

- **Tex**
  - Periwinkle grasshopper comb
  - Mint green cowboy hat
  - Blue bandana

1986-1987 Year 5

# Flutter Ponies
**(second set)**

The Flutter Ponies returned this year with what was advertised as a more secure wing setting (it wasn't any more secure, the wings still fell out). Lily and Rosedust also returned this year. Like the previous set of Flutter Ponies, some Flutter Ponies in this set have alternate head molds that are larger and have bigger eyes. Flutter Ponies were sold with a metallic or colored ribbon with metallic trim and a dual colored flower pick. They were packaged in a box with a plastic window. Prices below are for mint condition ponies with wings. Flutter Ponies in this set with out wings are worth $5 to $10.

$40 to $45

- **Cloud Puff**
    - Yellow with purple flower pick
    - Metallic ribbon (pink)
    - 2 wings

$40 to $45

- **Tropical Breeze**
    - Lavender with pink flower pick
    - Pink ribbon with gold trim
    - 2 wings

$40 to $45

- **Wind Drifter**
    - Pink with yellow flower pick
    - Pink ribbon with gold trim
    - 2 wings

$40 to $45

- **Wingsong**
    - Blue with yellow flower pick
    - Green ribbon with gold trim
    - 2 wings

# Pony Friends

The Pony Friends were a very unusual set. To start with, not a single creature in this set was a pony. They were four safari animals with pony-like faces. Secondly, some Pony Friends, instead of the traditional rump symbol, were covered in symbols. While First Tooth Baby Sundance appeared on the packaging for this set, she was never produced. Each Pony Friend came packaged on a bubble card with a brush or comb and a ribbon.

- **Creamsicle the Giraffe**
    - Blue ribbon
    - Pinkish purple flower brush

- **Kingsley the Lion**
    - Yellow ribbon
    - Blue moon comb

- **Spunky the Camel**
    - Orange ribbon
    - Light green crescent moon comb

- **Zig Zag the Zebra**
    - Mint green ribbon
    - Mint green butterfly brush

1986-1987 Year 5

# Newborn Twins

The Newborn Twins were a new type of Baby Pony altogether. Smaller than the traditional Baby Pony, their chubby faces identified them as infants. They were also the first store offered set of Baby Ponies that were not the children of past adult ponies. Though later sets of individual Newborns were released, this marked the first set of pony twins. The twins each had slight differences that allowed their owner to tell which was which. Newborn Twin sets with both ponies and accessories can be worth $25 or greater.

- ❑ **Dibbles**
- ❑ **Nibbles**
    - ❑ Aqua bassinet with yellow canopy
    - ❑ Aqua teddy bear brush
    - ❑ Yellow teddy bear brush
    - ❑ 2 white bottles
    - ❑ Aqua rattle with yellow top
    - ❑ Pink rattle with aqua top
    - ❑ Pink and white elastic (for rattles)
    - ❑ 2 white diapers
    - ❑ Newborn pony diaper box

$5 to $10 each

**Telling your twins apart**: Dibbles is orange with pink pink hair which easily fades white and a pink swan while Nibbles is pink with light orange hair and an orange swan.

$5 to $10 each

- ❑ **Doodles**
- ❑ **Noodles**
    - ❑ Yellow snail rocker
    - ❑ Aqua snail rocker
    - ❑ Purple teddy bear brush
    - ❑ Yellow teddy bear brush
    - ❑ Yellow dish with white inside
    - ❑ 2 aqua spoons
    - ❑ 2 white nightgowns with pink bows
    - (**Variation**: pink nightgowns)
    - ❑ 2 white bottles
    - ❑ 2 white diapers
    - ❑ Newborn pony diaper box

**Telling your twins apart**: Doodles is pink with pink hair while Noodles is light blue with blue hair.

- ❑ **Jangles**
- ❑ **Tangles**
    - ❑ Purple snail rocker
    - ❑ Pink snail rocker
    - ❑ Purple teddy bear brush
    - ❑ Pink teddy bear brush
    - ❑ Purple dish with yellow inside
    - ❑ 2 pink spoons
    - ❑ 2 pink nightgowns with green bows
    - (**Variation**: white nightgowns)
    - ❑ 2 white bottles
    - ❑ 2 white diapers
    - ❑ Newborn pony diaper box

$5 to $10 each

**Telling your twins apart**: Jangles and Tangles have the same body color and symbol, but Jangles has yellow hair while Tangles has white.

- ☐ **Milkweed**
- ☐ **Tumbleweed**
    - ☐ Purple bassinette with pink canopy
    - ☐ Purple teddy bear brush
    - ☐ Aqua teddy bear brush
    - ☐ Light pink rattle with white top
    - ☐ Purple rattle with aqua top
    - ☐ 2 white bottles
    - ☐ 2 white diapers
    - ☐ Newborn pony diaper box

**Telling your twins apart**: Milkweed and Tumbleweed are nearly identical except for their poses. Milkweed has her left hind leg lifted while Tumbleweed has all feet on the ground.

- ☐ **Rattles**
- ☐ **Tattles**
    - ☐ Pink stroller with purple awning
    - ☐ Pink teddy bear brush
    - ☐ Light green teddy bear brush
    - ☐ Light pink with white text BABY necklace
    - ☐ Light purple with pink text BABY necklace
    - ☐ 2 white bottles
    - ☐ 2 white diapers
    - ☐ Newborn pony diaper box

**Telling your twins apart**: Rattles and Tattles are nearly identical except for their poses. Rattles has her right front leg lifted and her head oriented to the right while Tattles has her left leg lifted and her head oriented to the left. Tattles also has a pudgier face.

- ☐ **Sniffles**
- ☐ **Snookums**
    - ☐ Aqua stroller with yellow awning
    - ☐ Aqua green teddy bear brush
    - ☐ White teddy bear brush
    - ☐ White with purple text BABY necklace
    - ☐ Yellow with aqua text BABY necklace
    - ☐ 2 white bottles
    - ☐ 2 white diapers
    - ☐ Newborn pony diaper box

**Telling your twins apart**: Sniffles is purple with pink hair and a pink mittens symbol while Snookums is pink with purple hair and a purple mittens symbol.

1986-1987 Year 5

# Princess Ponies with Bushwoolies

The Princess Ponies, featured in the animated series, were an unusual set. Instead of the usual painted symbol, they had raised bejeweled metallic symbols. They also had tinsel in their hair. In addition to princess hats, wands, sparkly combs, and unusual metallic trimmed ribbons, Princess Ponies each also came with a bushwoolie, wearing a crown. Though the bushwoolies had been main characters in the specials, movie and TV show, this was the only time they were available to purchase. Each set was sold in a box. Bushwollies by themselves are valued at $10 or greater. **Collector's Note:** The raised symbols of the Princess Ponies were subject to fading, peeling and scratching so take this into account when pricing.

$10 to $15

- ❑ **Princess Primrose**
- ❑ **Chumster** (yellow bushwollie)
    - ❑ Pink ribbon with metallic trim
    - ❑ Lavender glittery star pick
    - ❑ Purple glittery magic wand
    - ❑ Light pink butterflies and flowers princess hat with yellow metallic trimmed ribbons

$10 to $15

- ❑ **Princess Royal Blue**
- ❑ **Wishful** (pink bushwollie)
    - ❑ Aqua ribbon with metallic trim
    - ❑ Purple glittery star pick
    - ❑ Light purple glittery magic wand
    - ❑ Blue moon and stars princess hat with gold-trimmed pink ribbons

$10 to $15

- ❑ **Princess Serena**
- ❑ **Cheery** (light pink bushwollie)
    - ❑ Pink ribbon with metallic trim
    - ❑ Blue glittery star pick
    - ❑ Light lavender glittery magic wand
    - ❑ Aqua teardrops and hears princess hat with gold-trimmed pink ribbons

The My Little Pony G1 Collector's Inventory

$15 to $20

$10 to $15

- **Princess Sparkle**
- **Hugster** (green bushwollie)
    - Aqua ribbon with metallic trim
    - Bright pink glittery star pick
    - Aqua glittery magic wand
    - Pink butterfly and flowers princess hat with gold-trimmed yellow ribbons

- **Princess Starburst**
- **Eager** (purple bushwollie)
    - White ribbon with metallic trim
    - Aqua glittery star pick
    - Pink glittery magic wand (**Variation**: light pink magic wand)
    - Yellow moons and stars princess hat with gold-trimmed pink ribbons

- **Princess Tiffany**
- **Friendly** (blue bushwollie)
    - White ribbon with metallic trim
    - Pale pink glittery star pick
    - Blue glittery magic wand
    - Purple teardrops and hearts princess hat with gold-trimmed yellow ribbons

$10 to $15

60

1986-1987 Year 5

# Sea Sparkle Baby Sea Ponies

The Sea Sparkle Baby Sea Ponies were the first Sea Ponies to have a symbol. Instead of on their rumps, however, their symbols were painted necklaces around their neck. They also each came with an animal shaped float like all Baby Sea Pony sets before them. Each Sea Sparkle Baby Sea Pony came packaged on a bubble card with a fish comb and ribbon. Prices below do not include floats. Sea Pony floats are worth $5 to $10 even with out the pony.

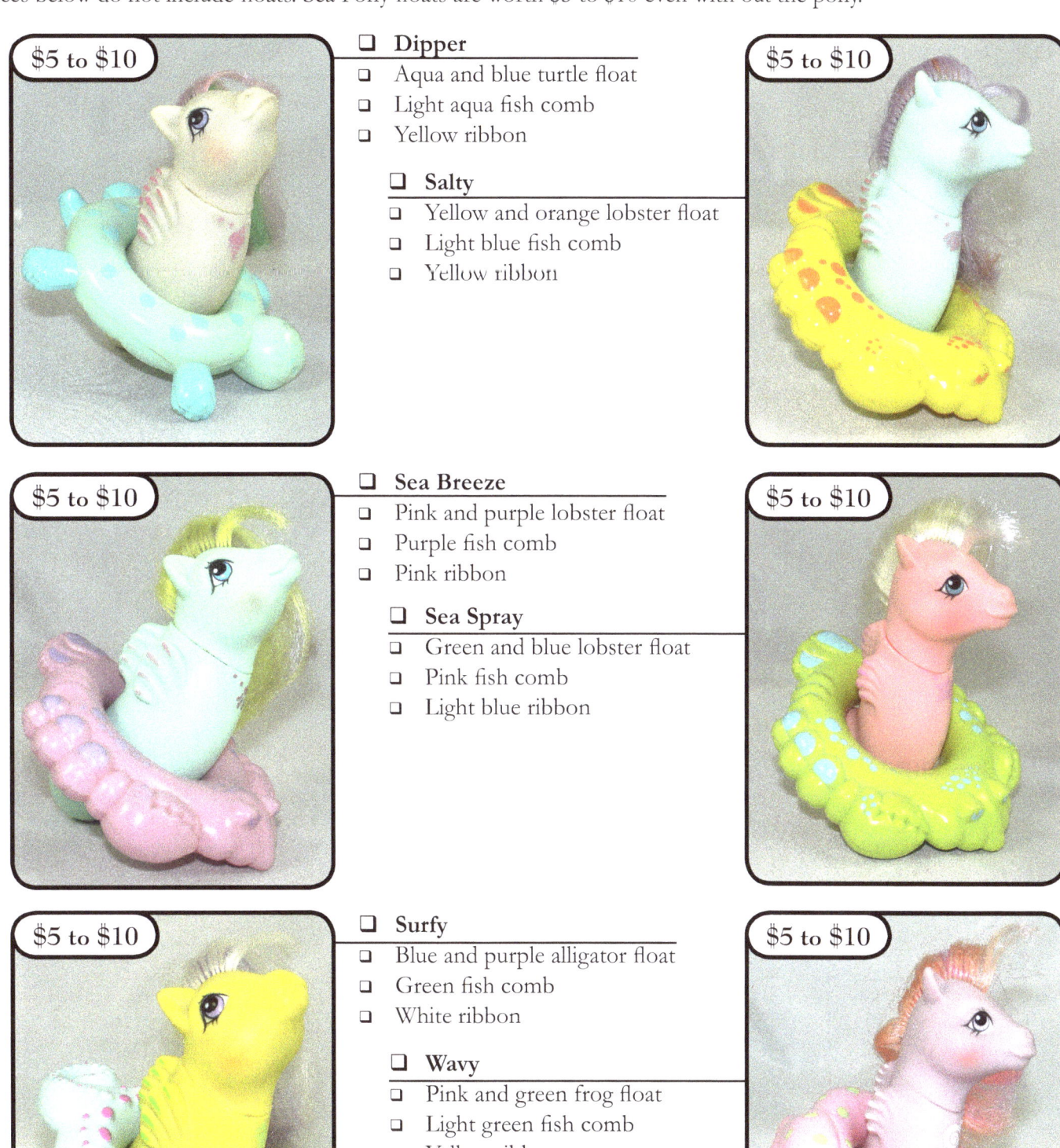

- **Dipper**
  - Aqua and blue turtle float
  - Light aqua fish comb
  - Yellow ribbon

- **Salty**
  - Yellow and orange lobster float
  - Light blue fish comb
  - Yellow ribbon

- **Sea Breeze**
  - Pink and purple lobster float
  - Purple fish comb
  - Pink ribbon

- **Sea Spray**
  - Green and blue lobster float
  - Pink fish comb
  - Light blue ribbon

- **Surfy**
  - Blue and purple alligator float
  - Green fish comb
  - White ribbon

- **Wavy**
  - Pink and green frog float
  - Light green fish comb
  - Yellow ribbon

The My Little Pony G1 Collector's Inventory

# So-Soft Ponies
**(second set)**

The second set of So-Soft Ponies is lesser known than the first as they were not featured characters on the television show, but they still had the same soft flocked bodies of their predecessors. Each So-Soft Pony came packaged on a bubble card with either a brush or comb, and a ribbon.

$15 to $20

- **Angel**
  - Dark turquoise sun pick
  - Orange ribbon

$15 to $20

- **Bangles**
  - Purple flower brush
  - Pink ribbon

$30 to $35

- **Crumpet**
  - Blue crescent moon comb
  - Dark reddish pink ribbon

$15 to $20

- **Taffy**
  - Blue flower brush
  - Yellow ribbon

$15 to $20

- **Twilight**
  - Yellow crescent moon comb
  - White ribbon

1986-1987 Year 5

# Slumber Party Gift Pack

Like the Party Pack, the Slumber Party Gift Pack was a sampler of all the new pony sets that had been introduced in the past year. In addition to five ponies, the set also came with a large assortment of accessories to keep your ponies partying all night! Accessories from this set are hard to find and highly sought after. The accessories can be worth $25 or more even with out the ponies. Price listed is for mint condition Pink Dreams with wings. With out, she is valued at $10 to $15.

$5 to $10 — **Nightcap** (First Tooth Baby Pony)

$5 to $10 — **Pillow Talk** (Twice As Fancy Pony)

$35 to $40 — **Pink Dreams** (Flutter Pony)

$5 to $10 each — **Sleep Tight** (Newborn Twin)   **Sleepy Head** (Newborn Twin)

**Telling your Newborn Twins apart:** Sleep Tight has a pink body with blue hair and a baby carriage symbol. Sleepy Head has a blue body with a striped PJs symbol and pink hair.

- 6 nightcaps
  - Pink/blue/green stripes with pink trim [Pillow Talk]
  - Pink/green/yellow stars with yellow trim [Nightcap]
  - Pink/yellow/blue flowers with green stems and mint green trim [Pink Dreams]
  - Pink striped with purple trim [Sleepy Head]
  - Pink striped with purple trim [Sleep Tight]
- 2 pairs of pink striped panties
- 2 party panties diaper boxes
- Sleeping bag
- Tub of popcorn (featuring Cherries Jubilee)
- Box of cookies
- Green cloud-shaped record player with moon arm
- Pink record
- Record sleeve picturing a rock star pony
- Green phone (with pink receiver)
- Green television set (featuring Truly)
- Pink milk carton

The My Little Pony G1 Collector's Inventory

- Issue of the full color "Teen" magazine (pony edition)
- Issue of the full color "Screen" magazine (pony edition)
- "Rainbow Hop" game (like Twister)
- Game spinner
- 5 hair ribbons
- Blue shooting stars comb

## Soft and Sleepy Newborns

The Soft and Sleepy Newborns are often hard to find because many sellers do not realize that they are part of the My Little Pony family. They were large, almost 12 inches tall, with Beddy Bye style eyes that close when they are placed on their sides to sleep or when their tails are brushed or pulled. Each Soft and Sleepy Newborn Pony came dressed in a bonnet and matching panties. Each was packaged in a box with a plastic window with a pacifier and a special hand-held brush. Complete with all accessories, ponies in this set are valued at $60 or more.

$35 to $40

- Hushabye
    - Pink bonnet
    - Pink panties
    - Blue pacifier
    - Pink oval grooming brush

1986-1987 Year 5

- **Pink Dreams**
  - Blue bonnet
  - Blue panties
  - Aqua pacifier
  - Blue oval grooming brush

- **Sweet Dreams**
  - White bonnet
  - White panties
  - White pacifier
  - Purple oval grooming brush

65

# Twinkle Eyed Ponies
**(second set)**

"Her eyes sparkle and shine like precious jewels." The second set of Twinkle-Eyed Ponies had jeweled eyes like their predecessors, but are generally harder to find and more sought after by collectors than other Twinkle-Eyed Ponies. Mimic is especially popular with collectors and commands a higher price than the others in this set. Each pony was packaged with a brush or comb and a ribbon on a bubble card.

**Bright Eyes** — $10 to $15
- Yellow shooting stars comb
- Bright orange ribbon

**Locket** — $10 to $15
- Purple sun pick
- Dark pink ribbon

**Mimic** — $75 & up
- Light pink shooting star brush
- Bright yellow ribbon

**Quackers** — $10 to $15
- Orange sun pick
- Bright blue ribbon

**Tic-Tac-Toe** — $10 to $15
- Dark pink shooting star brush
- Mint green ribbon

1986-1987 Year 5

# Twice As Fancy Ponies

"The most beautiful ponies in Ponyland!" Twice As Fancy Ponies, which collectors usually abbreviate as TAF, were different from other ponies in the past because instead of simply having a single symbol on their rump, they had symbols covering their bodies, including their forehead or cheek. Each came packaged on a bubble card with a brush or a comb and a ribbon.

$5 to $10

- **Dancing Butterflies**
  - Pink sun pick (**Variation**: purple sun comb)
  - White ribbon (**Variation**: blue ribbon)

- **Love Melody**
  - Pink butterfly brush
  - Pink ribbon (**Variation**: pale purple ribbon)

- **Milky Way**
  - Blue butterfly brush
  - Pinkish purple ribbon

- **Sugarberry**
  - Pink sun pick
  - Green ribbon

- **Sweet Tooth**
  - Purple crescent moon comb
  - Pink ribbon

- **Up, Up, and Away**
  - Green crescent moon comb
  - Yellow ribbon

67

# 1987-1988
## Year 6

Many popular pony sets, such as the Princess Ponies, Big Brother Ponies, Newborn Twins, and Twice As Fancy Ponies, made encore performances in Year 6 with new friends. In addition, many new sets were available that showcased special features like scented bodies, growing tails, and ponies whose symbols or body color magically changed right before your eyes. Year 6 is also the start of the most prolific years in MLP history with 1987 to 1990 being the years that saw the most ponies released.

# Big Brother Ponies
## (second set)

Three ponies from the previous set of Big Brother Ponies returned this year with three new ponies. Each Big Brother Pony was sold on a bubble card with a hat, bandana, and a brush or comb. Salty, Steamer and Tex were also released but they were identical to their previous issue. Big Brother Ponies with hats and bandanas are worth over double the prices listed below.

$15 to $20

$15 to $20

- **Barnacle**
    - Pirate hat with molded eye patch
    - Dark yellow bandanna
    - Yellow puppy brush

- **Chief**
    - Red fire fighter helmet
    - Yellow bandanna
    - Blue racecar comb

- **Wig Wam**
    - Yellow feathered headdress
    - Blue bandanna
    - Red racecar comb

$15 to $20

1987-1988 Year 6

# Brush 'n Grow Ponies

The Brush 'n Grow Ponies had multicolored long manes and a special tail that could be pulled out to twice its length or cranked back to a shorter length by turning the pony's head from side to side. All their symbols were related to hair care. They came packaged in a box with a matching long brush and comb set and barrettes.

$10 to $15

$10 to $15

- **Braided Beauty**
    - Mint hearts and dots long brush
    - Yellow hearts and dots long comb
    - 2 wide pink ribbons
    - White shooting star barrette
    - Purple hearts barrette

- **Bouquet**
    - Purple hearts and dots long brush
    - Blue hearts and dots long comb
    - 2 wide dark pink ribbons
    - Light purple shooting star barrette
    - Pink hearts barrette

$10 to $15

$10 to $15

- **Curly Locks**
    - Yellow hearts and dots long brush
    - Hot pink hearts and dots long comb
    - 2 wide blue ribbons
    - Dark purple shooting star barrette
    - White hearts barrette

- **Pretty Vision**
    - Dark pink hearts and dots long brush
    - Aqua hearts and dots long comb
    - 2 wide pink ribbons
    - Blue shooting star barrette
    - Green hearts barrette

The My Little Pony G1 Collector's Inventory

- **Ringlets**
    - Light purple hearts and dots long brush
    - Aqua hearts and dots long comb
    - 2 wide purple ribbons
    - Pink shooting star barrette
    - Blue hearts barrette

- **Twisty Tail**
    - Blue hearts and dots long brush
    - Orange hearts and dots long comb
    - 2 wide white ribbons
    - Green shooting star barrette
    - Yellow hearts barrette

## Happy Tails Ponies

The hallmark of Happy Tails Ponies was their swishing tails. When hugged (squeezed with your fingers), an inside mechanism would cause their tails to twirl to show their love for you. A molded ring around their tail allows it to move freely from side to side. (**Collector's Note**: A common problem with ponies in this set was the tail twirling mechanism getting turned around so that you would have to hug their underbellies instead of their sides to get them to work.) Happy Tails Ponies were made of softer, squishier plastic than other ponies making them easier to squeeze. The ponies in this set came with squirrel shaped tail clips and bird hair picks with brightly colored hair extensions. Each pony's symbol had two animals hugging or playing. Each Happy Tails Pony came packaged in a box with a brush or comb and ribbon.

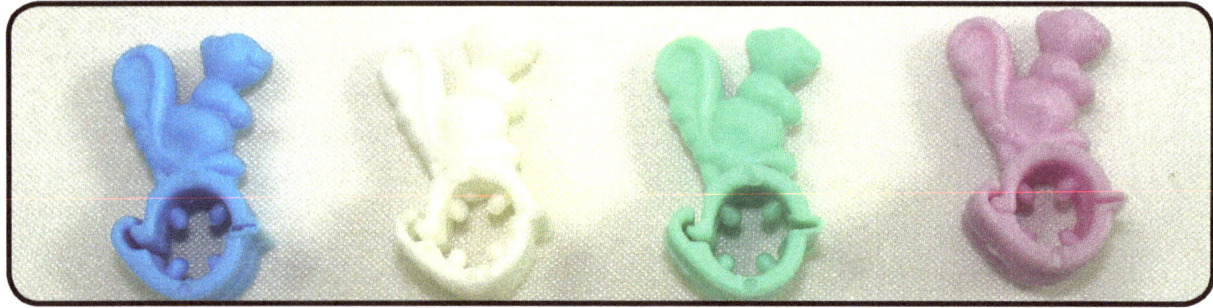

1987-1988 Year 6

$5 to $10

- **Romper**
  - Dark pink bird pick with chartreuse hair
  - Blue squirrel tail clip
  - Dark pink sun pick
  - Yellow ribbon

- **Squeezer**
  - White bird pick with blue hair
  - Dark pink squirrel tail clip
  - Blue duck comb
  - Yellow ribbon

$5 to $10

- **Tabby**
  - Dark aqua bird pick with yellow hair
  - White squirrel tail clip
  - Blue butterfly brush
  - Pink ribbon

- **Tall Tales**
  - Yellow bird pick with dark pink hair
  - White squirrel tail clip
  - Lavender bird brush
  - Pinkish purple ribbon

$5 to $10

- **Tossles**
  - Dark blue bird pick with red hair
  - Lavender squirrel tail clip
  - Aqua flower brush
  - White ribbon

- **Woosie**
  - Purple bird pick with pink hair
  - Dark aqua squirrel tail clip
  - Yellow flower comb
  - Pink ribbon

$5 to $10

$5 to $10

73

# Magic Message Ponies

Magic Message Ponies looked like a standard earth pony, unicorn, or pegasus until you applied heat by touching or gently rubbing their symbols. With the change in temperature, their symbol would fade away to reveal a secret image underneath. When the symbol cooled, it returned to the original symbol. Magic Message Ponies also had a matching cheek symbol. (**Collector's Note**: Over time, many Magic Message Ponies' symbols lost the ability to transform or remained permanently on one of the two images. Their symbols were also more prone to scratching or fading than other symbols.) Each pony came packaged on a bubble card with a brush or comb and a ribbon.

$5 to $10

- **Cloud Dreamer**
  - Periwinkle shooting star brush
  - Yellow ribbon

$5 to $10

- **Cuddles**
  - Light purple teddy bear brush
  - White ribbon

$5 to $10

- **Floater**
  - Green bird brush
  - Pink ribbon

$5 to $10

- **Magic Hat**
  - Blue butterfly brush (**Variation**: purple star brush)
  - Light blue ribbon

$5 to $10

- **Mirror Mirror**
  - Pink crescent moon comb (**Variation**: yellow flower brush)
  - Peach ribbon (**Variation**: green ribbon)

$5 to $10

- **Windy**
  - Yellow flower brush
  - Green ribbon

1987-1988 Year 6

# Newborn Twins
**(second set)**

Like the first set of Newborn Twins, these siblings also had the smaller newborn body design. This was the second, and final, set of Newborn Twins. Each set of twins had identical symbols. Some twins also shared hair and body colors, while others had different hair and body colors. Each Newborn Twins set came packaged in a box with a variety of accessories. Newborn Twin sets are worth are worth $15 to $20 unless otherwise marked.

$5 to $10 each

❑ Big Top
❑ Toppy
  ❑ Yellow teddy bear brush
  ❑ Purple teddy bear brush
  ❑ Purple sandbox
  ❑ Yellow dish with white inside
  ❑ 2 aqua spoons
  ❑ 2 white baby bottles
  ❑ 2 blue ribbons
  ❑ 2 white diapers
  ❑ Newborn pony diaper box

**Telling your twins apart**: Big Top is white with yellow hair while Toppy is yellow with white hair.

❑ Jabber
❑ Jebber
  ❑ Light green teddy bear brush
  ❑ Light pink teddy bear brush
  ❑ Pink sandbox
  ❑ Light pink with white text BABY necklace
  ❑ Light purple with pink text BABY necklace
  ❑ 2 white baby bottles
  ❑ 2 pink ribbons
  ❑ 2 white diapers
  ❑ Newborn pony diaper box

$5 to $10 each

**Telling your twins apart**: Nearly identical except for their poses. Jabber's right front leg is lifted and her head oriented to the right while Jebber has her left leg lifted and her head oriented to the left. Jebber also has a pudgier face.

$5 to $10 each

❑ Puddles
❑ Peeks
  ❑ Aqua and pink seesaw (**Variations**: pink with yellow or yellow with aqua seesaw)
  ❑ Yellow teddy bear brush
  ❑ Pink teddy bear brush
  ❑ Light pink rattle with white top
  ❑ Purple rattle with aqua top
  ❑ Pink elastic
  ❑ Light blue elastic
  ❑ 2 white baby bottles
  ❑ 2 ribbons
  ❑ 2 white diapers
  ❑ Newborn pony diaper box

**Telling your twins apart**: Nearly identical except for their poses. Peeks has her right front leg lifted while Puddles has all feet on the ground.

$10 to $15 each     $30 to $35 set

**Telling your twins apart**: Sandcastle is orange with blue hair while Shovels is blue with orange hair.

- ❑ Sandcastle
- ❑ Shovels
    - ❑ Pink snail rocker
    - ❑ Purple snail rocker
    - ❑ White teddy bear brush
    - ❑ Aqua teddy bear brush
    - ❑ Yellow with aqua text BABY necklace
    - ❑ White with purple text BABY necklace
    - ❑ 2 white bottles
    - ❑ Dark yellow ribbons
    - ❑ 2 white diapers
    - ❑ Newborn pony diaper box

- ❑ Speckles
- ❑ Bunkie
    - ❑ Aqua snail rocker
    - ❑ Yellow snail rocker
    - ❑ Aqua teddy bear brush
    - ❑ Yellow teddy bear brush
    - ❑ Light pink rattle with yellow top
    - ❑ Aqua rattle with yellow top
    - ❑ 2 white baby bottles
    - ❑ 2 light green ribbons
    - ❑ 2 white diapers
    - ❑ Newborn pony diaper box

$5 to $10 each

**Telling your twins apart**: Speckles is purple with yellow hair while Bunkie is yellow with purple hair.

$5 to $10 each

**Telling your twins apart**: Their body types and symbols are the same but Sticky has white hair while Sniffles has blue hair.

- ❑ Sticky
- ❑ Sniffles
    - ❑ Pink with yellow seesaw (**Variations**: aqua with pink or a yellow with aqua seesaw)
    - ❑ Aqua teddy bear brush
    - ❑ Purple teddy bear brush
    - ❑ Purple dish with yellow inside
    - ❑ 2 light pink spoons
    - ❑ 2 white baby bottles
    - ❑ 2 white diapers
    - ❑ Newborn pony diaper box

1987-1988 Year 6

# Peek-A-Boo Baby Ponies

The Peek-A-Boo Baby Ponies were the first set of ponies that could turn their heads. Little boy ponies in this set had Clydesdale hooves like Big Brother Ponies. Some ponies in this set also had their first tooth. None of the ponies in this set were the offspring of ponies in any other sets. Peek-a-boo Baby Ponies came packaged in a box with a special bib with colored trim, a duck comb or teddy bear brush and a ribbon.

$5 to $10

- **Baby Graffiti**
  - Butterfly bib with pink trim
  - Purple duck comb
  - Dark yellow ribbon

- **Baby Noddins**
  - Butterfly bib with aqua trim
  - Dark pink teddy bear brush
  - Dark yellow ribbon

$5 to $10

$10 to $15

- **Baby Ribbs**
  - Teddy bear bib with purple trim
  - Purple duck comb
  - Pink ribbon

- **Baby Snippy**
  - Butterfly bib with purple trim
  - Aqua duck comb
  - Light blue ribbon

$5 to $10

$5 to $10

- **Baby Sweet Stuff**
  - Butterfly bib with blue trim
  - Yellow teddy bear brush
  - White ribbon

- **Baby Whirly-Twirl**
  - Teddy bear bib with yellow trim
  - Blue teddy bear brush
  - Purple ribbon

$10 to $15

The My Little Pony G1 Collector's Inventory

# Pony Friends
### (second set)

"Baby animal pals for your ponies!" The Pony Friends returned in a second set with Creamsicle and Kingsley unchanged. This set was harder to find than the previous and is usually worth more today. The manes and tails of the Pony Friends were brushable with the exception of Cutesaurus, who only had a brushable mane. Each Pony Friend came packaged in a box with a flower or butterfly brush and a ribbon. Pony Friends of this set fall in and out of favor with collectors so their prices are particularly volatile and can vary widely above and below what is listed.

$30 to $35

❑ **Cha Cha the Llama**
  ❑ Light blue ribbon
  ❑ Purple flower brush

$20 to $25

❑ **Cutesaurus the Dinosaur**
  ❑ Light blue ribbon
  ❑ Blue flower brush

$20 to $25

❑ **Edgar the Elephant**
  ❑ Light aqua ribbon
  ❑ Turquoise butterfly brush

$30 to $35

❑ **Oakly the Moose**
  ❑ Purple pink ribbon
  ❑ Blue butterfly brush

1987-1988 Year 6

# Princess Ponies
### (second set)

The second set of Princess Ponies came with wands, jeweled raised symbols, and tinsel in their manes and tails like the first set. However, unlike the first set, they did not come with bushwoolies and, instead of damsel hats, this set came with crown-shaped barrettes. Each Princess Pony was packaged in a box. Prices listed below are for loose, mint condition ponies. Princess Ponies of this set are worth $50 or more with accessories.

$10 to $15

$10 to $15

- ❑ **Princess Dawn**
    - ❑ Light green wand
    - ❑ Yellow oval-shaped crown
    - ❑ Aqua glittery star pick
    - ❑ Yellow ribbon with metallic trim

- ❑ **Princess Misty**
    - ❑ Light aqua wand
    - ❑ Blue 3 point circle crown
    - ❑ Yellow glittery star pick
    - ❑ Turquoise ribbon with metallic trim

$10 to $15

$10 to $15

- ❑ **Princess Moondust**
    - ❑ Pale pink wand (**Variation**: pink wand)
    - ❑ Dark aqua 3 point circle crown
    - ❑ Dark purple glittery star pick
    - ❑ White ribbon with metallic trim

- ❑ **Princess Pristina**
    - ❑ Raspberry pink wand
    - ❑ Pink 3 point diamond crown
    - ❑ Blue glittery star pick
    - ❑ Pinkish purple ribbon with metallic trim

- **Princess Sunbeam**
    - Dark blue wand
    - Purple oval-shaped crown
    - Light aqua glittery star pick
    - Lavender ribbon with metallic trim

- **Princess Taffeta**
    - Yellow wand
    - Purple 3 point diamond crown
    - Aqua glittery star pick
    - Dark pink ribbon with metallic trim

# Summer Wing Ponies

The Summer Wing Ponies were a completely new type of pony. Only a little smaller than a baby pony, they had thinner faces and butterfly-like multi colored wings. Unlike the Flutter Ponies, these wings could not flap and were more securely fastened. Summer Wing Ponies all had symbols that are either birds or flying insects. They had a small symbol on either their cheek or forehead. Each Summer Wing Pony was packaged in a box with a flowered pick and a colored metallic ribbon.

- **Buzzer**
    - Metallic blue hair ribbon
    - Pink flower pick

1987-1988 Year 6

$10 to $15

- **Glow**
  - Metallic blue hair ribbon
  - Dark pink flower pick

- **High Flier**
  - Metallic gold hair ribbon
  - Yellow flower pick

$10 to $15

$10 to $15

- **Lady Flutter**
  - Metallic pink hair ribbon
  - Dark aqua flower pick

- **Little Flitter**
  - Metallic gold hair ribbon
  - Light pink flower pick

$10 to $15

$10 to $15

- **Sky Dancer**
  - Metallic pink hair ribbon
  - Lavender flower pick

# Sundae Best Ponies

The Sundae Best Ponies were the first set of ponies whose feature was a scent. Each pony in this set had a raised symbol in the shape of an ice cream confection and was scented to smell like that treat. Each Sundae Best Pony was packaged on a bubble card with either a candy wrapper comb or lollipop brush and a barrette.

- **Banana Surprise**
  - Purple ice cream cone barrette
  - Pinkish-purple wrapped candy comb

- **Coco Berry**
  - Mint green lollipop barrette
  - Purple wrapped candy comb

- **Crunch Berry**
  - Pink ice cream cone barrette
  - Aqua lollipops brush

- **Peppermint Crunch**
  - Yellow sundae barrette
  - Blue lollipops brush

- **Sherbet**
  - Yellow sundae barrette
  - Mint green lollipops brush

- **Swirly Whirly**
  - Dark pink lollipop barrette
  - Pale pink wrapped candy comb

$5 to $10 (each)

# Sweetberry Ponies

1987-1988 Year 6

The Sweetberry Ponies were scented, like the Sundae Best Ponies, but they were scented like berries rather than ice cream. Sweetberry Ponies had symbols that were berry themed. Each Sweetberry Pony was packaged on a bubble card with a flower brush or sun comb and a ribbon.

- **Blueberry Baskets**
  - Purple ribbon
  - Yellow sun pick

- **Boysenberry Pie**
  - White ribbon
  - Pink flower brush

- **Cherry Treats**
  - Pink ribbon
  - Aqua flower brush

- **Cranberry Muffins**
  - Orange yellow ribbon
  - Pink sun pick

- **Raspberry Jam**
  - Blue ribbon
  - Purple flower brush

- **Strawberry Surprise**
  - Light blue ribbon
  - Green sun pick

$5 to $10 (each)

The My Little Pony G1 Collector's Inventory

# Twice-As-Fancy Ponies
### (second set)

When the Twice-As-Fancy Ponies returned for a second time, they were much harder to find than the first set and are consequently worth more today. Just like the first set, these ponies had symbols all over their body and on their cheek or forehead, though this set did not come with stickers. Each set came packaged on a bubble card with a brush or comb and a ribbon.

$20 to $25

- **Bonnie Bonnets**
  - Dark blue butterfly brush
  - Dark blue ribbon

- **Buttons**
  - Blue butterfly brush
  - Pink ribbon

$25 to $30

$15 to $20

- **Merriweather**
  - Purple crescent moon comb
  - Pink ribbon

- **Munchy**
  - Light green sun pick
  - Orange ribbon

$35 to $40

$20 to $25

- **Night Glider**
  - Yellow moon comb
  - Yellow ribbon

- **Yum Yum**
  - Dark pink sun pick
  - Purple ribbon

$15 to $20

1987-1988 Year 6

# Watercolor Baby Sea Ponies

The Watercolor Baby Sea Ponies, the last set of Sea Ponies ever released, had hair that changed color when placed in warm water. (**Collector's Note:** With time, they lose their color change ability.) Watercolor Baby Sea Ponies had soft, cottony hair. Each Watercolor Baby Sea Pony was sold on a bubble card with a float, a fish comb, and a ribbon. Prices below are for ponies loose, without floats. Floats are valued at $5 to $10.

$5 to $10

- **Foamy**
  - Blue/yellow frog float
  - Pink fish comb
  - Orange ribbon

$5 to $10

- **Misty**
  - Purple/orange duck float
  - Lavender fish comb
  - Blue ribbon

$5 to $10

- **Sealight**
  - Green/pink turtle float
  - Yellow fish comb
  - Pink ribbon

$5 to $10

- **Seashore**
  - Orange/blue fish float
  - Blue fish comb
  - Pink ribbon

$5 to $10

- **Seawinkle**
  - Pink/green alligator float
  - Magenta fish comb
  - Pink ribbon

$5 to $10

- **Wavedancer**
  - Yellow/purple lobster float
  - Green fish comb
  - Yellow ribbon

# 1988-1989
## Year 7

Year 7 introduced a multitude of new sets all sporting different themes and characteristics. Ponies were available with candy and perfume scents, fluffy and color changing hair, ornate carousel designs, shimmering glitter, and the ability to dance.

# Baby Fancy Pants Ponies

The Baby Fancy Pants Ponies were another set that altered the traditional symbol design. These ponies each wore a pair of fancy panties that served as their symbol decal and each came with a colored mesh-like bow to wear around their necks. Each came packaged in a box with many of the baby accessories that originated with previous sets.

$5 to $10

### ❑ Baby Bows
- ❑ Purple neck bow
- ❑ Duck pull toy
- ❑ Sippy cup
- ❑ Yellow dish
- ❑ Purple spoon
- ❑ Pink ribbon
- ❑ Aqua duck com

$5 to $10

### ❑ Baby Dots 'n Hearts
- ❑ Purple-pink neck bow
- ❑ Stack toy
- ❑ Sippy cup
- ❑ Aqua-blue dish
- ❑ Pink spoon
- ❑ Yellow ribbon
- ❑ Yellow bird brush

$5 to $10

### ❑ Baby Glider
- ❑ Hot pink neck bow
- ❑ Duck pull toy
- ❑ Turquoise dish
- ❑ Dark pink spoon
- ❑ Yellow ribbon
- ❑ Green duck comb

$5 to $10

### ❑ Baby Splashes
- ❑ Green neck bow
- ❑ Stack toy
- ❑ Sippy cup
- ❑ Lime green dish
- ❑ Yellow spoon
- ❑ White ribbon
- ❑ Blue bird brush

1988-1989 Year 7

- ❏ **Baby Starburst**
    - ❏ Yellow neck bow
    - ❏ Stack toy
    - ❏ Sippy cup
    - ❏ Blue dish
    - ❏ Yellow spoon
    - ❏ Purple ribbon
    - ❏ Yellow duck comb

- ❏ **Baby Sunnybunch**
    - ❏ Pink neck bow
    - ❏ Duck pull toy
    - ❏ Sippy cup
    - ❏ Blue dish
    - ❏ Pink spoon
    - ❏ Pink ribbon
    - ❏ Purple bird brush

# Baby Ponies & Pretty Pals

"Pretty baby pony and playful animal friend!" The boxed Baby Ponies & Pretty Pals set paired a baby pony with an animal similar to a Pony Friend. The pony and its pal had matching symbols and came with a variety of great accessories to play with.

- ❏ **Baby Fleecy**
- ❏ **Baby Woolley the Lamb**
    - ❏ Aqua wagon with yellow wheels and handle
    - ❏ Stack toy
    - ❏ Small pink bottle
    - ❏ Dark aqua teddy bear brush
    - ❏ Pink duck comb
    - ❏ Blue ribbon

89

- **Baby Lucky Leaf**
- **Baby Leafy the Calf**
  - Pink sandbox
  - Light aqua-blue dish
  - Pink spoon
  - Yellow spoon
  - Small green bottle
  - Pink teddy bear brush
  - Dark pink duck comb
  - Pink ribbon

$15 to $20     $15 to $20

$10 to $15     $5 to $10

- **Baby Pockets**
- **Baby Hoppy the Kangaroo**
  - Orange wagon with pink wheels and handle
  - Stack toy
  - Small pink bottle
  - Green teddy bear brush
  - Blue duck comb
  - Light green ribbon

- **Baby Stripes**
- **Baby Nectar the Panda**
  - Light purple sandbox
  - Yellow dish
  - Pink spoon
  - Aqua spoon
  - Small aqua bottle
  - Pink teddy bear brush
  - Yellow duck comb
  - Yellow ribbon

$10 to $15     $5 to $10

# Candy Cane Ponies

1988-1989 Year 7

The Candy Cane Ponies, like the Sweetberry and Sundae Best Ponies before them, were scented like the yummy treat they were named after. However, as an added bonus, their striped hair came in tight curls forming neat peppermint sticks in their mane and tails. Each Candy Cane Pony was packaged in a box with a wrapped candy comb and barrette.

$5 to $10

❑ **Caramel Crunch**
  ❑ Pink lollipop barrette
  ❑ Aqua wrapped candy comb
  ❑ Green ribbon

$5 to $10

❑ **Lemon Treats**
  ❑ Purple lollipop barrette
  ❑ Pink wrapped candy comb
  ❑ Yellow ribbon

$5 to $10

❑ **Mint Dreams**
  ❑ Yellow ice cream cone barrette
  ❑ Purple wrapped candy comb
  ❑ Light pink ribbon

$5 to $10

❑ **Molasses**
  ❑ Pink sundae barrette
  ❑ Purple wrapped candy comb
  ❑ Light green ribbon

$5 to $10

❑ **Sugar Apple**
  ❑ Light pink sundae barrette
  ❑ Yellow wrapped candy comb
  ❑ Pink ribbon

$5 to $10

❑ **Sugar Sweet**
  ❑ Purple ice cream cone barrette
  ❑ Periwinkle wrapped candy comb
  ❑ Dark pink ribbon

# Dance 'n Prance Ponies

Dance 'n Prance Ponies were the only set of US G1 ponies ever made that could move on their own. Each pony, posed with their head facing upwards, had a flower shaped knob on her chest. Once wound, the pony's tail twirled very quickly causing her to vibrate and dance around. The top of each pony's tail came encased in a plastic sleeve to protect it while spinning and the ponies themselves came with a large number of accessories. Each Dance 'n Prance Pony was packaged in a box with a shooting star brush or star comb, a pair of earrings, a gold mesh ribbon, a bow clip with attached colored hair, a bird and flower barrette, and a boa. **Collector's Note**: The knob should, when wound, get tight and the pony's tail should spin very quickly once released, causing her body to move around like dancing. If the knob is very easy to turn, unable to turn at all (overwound) or if the tail spins slowly or all in one quick burst, your pony is likely broken.

- ☐ **D.J.**
    - ☐ Wide gold mesh ribbon
    - ☐ White boa
    - ☐ Pink earrings with dark pink gems
    - ☐ Dark pink bird and lily barrette
    - ☐ Aqua hair clip with pink hair and blue tinsel
    - ☐ Lavender shooting star brush

- ☐ **Player**
    - ☐ Wide gold mesh ribbon
    - ☐ Pink boa
    - ☐ Yellow earrings with pink gems
    - ☐ Blue hair clip with dark pink hair and gold tinsel
    - ☐ Light blue bird and lily barrette
    - ☐ Yellow stars comb

1988-1989 Year 7

- **Songster**
  - Wide gold mesh ribbon
  - Aqua boa
  - White earrings with purple gems
  - Yellow hair clip with red hair and silver tinsel
  - Red bird and lily barrette
  - Blue/aqua shooting star brush

- **Swinger**
  - Wide gold mesh ribbon
  - White boa
  - White earrings with blue gems
  - Yellow hair clip with blue hair/multicolor tinsel
  - Dark blue bird and lily barrette
  - Pink shooting star brush

- **Tap Dancer**
  - Wide gold mesh ribbon
  - Pink boa
  - Pink earrings with aqua gems
  - Pink hair clip with aqua hair and gold tinsel
  - Pale pink bird and lily barrette
  - Mint green stars comb

- **Twirler**
  - Wide gold mesh ribbon
  - Aqua boa
  - Purple hair clip with yellow hair and gold tinsel
  - Aqua earrings with pink gems
  - Light yellow bird and lily barrette
  - Blue stars comb

The My Little Pony G1 Collector's Inventory

# Loving Family Ponies

The Loving Family Ponies were pony sets that came with a mommy (earth pony), a daddy (Big Brother style pony) and a baby boy or girl pony. The daddy and the mommy ponies had unique symbols, but the baby's symbols were a combination of both parents. Each Loving Family Pony set was sold in a box with a flower brush, a flower pick, and three ribbons.

$5 to $10 each

- ❑ **Daddy Apple Delight**
- ❑ **Baby Daughter Apple Delight**
- ❑ **Mommy Apple Delight**
- ❑ 3 blue ribbons
- ❑ Pink flower brush
- ❑ Yellow flower pick

$5 to $10 each

1988-1989 Year 7

- **Mommy Bright Bouquet**
- **Baby Daughter Bright Bouquet**
- **Daddy Bright Bouquet**
- 3 pink ribbons
- Purple flower brush
- Blue flower pick

$5 to $10 each

- **Daddy Sweet Celebrations**
- **Baby Son Sweet Celebrations**
- **Mommy Sweet Celebrations**
- 3 pinkish-purple ribbon
- Green flower pick
- Pink flower brush

## Megan & Twice As Fancy Sundance

Megan and Sundance made their final appearance this year. This time however, both characters were dramatically different. Megan had a larger head and Sundance not only changed poses, but was now a Twice As Fancy Pony. Megan came dressed in a white dress with Sundance's symbols printed all over it. Both Megan and Twice As Fancy Sundance have a color changing steak in their hair just like the Sunshine Ponies that changes color in sunlight. **Collector's Note:** There is a variation of this Megan with bangs.

- **Megan** (larger head)
- **Sundance** (Twice As Fancy)
- Dress patterned with Sundance's symbol
- Panties
- Dark pink slip-on shoes
- Pink standard comb
- Pink ribbon

$10 to $15

$10 to $15

# Merry-Go-Round Ponies

The Merry-Go-Round Ponies, instead of the traditional symbol design, had fanciful molded saddle blankets on their back that gave them the appearance of carousel horses. Merry-Go-Round Ponies were packaged in a box with a flower brush. This set did not come packaged with ribbons.

- **Brilliant Blossoms**
  - Blue flower brush
- **Diamond Dreams**
  - Purple flower brush
- **Flower Bouquet**
  - Dark mint green flower brush
- **Sparkler**
  - Yellow flower brush
- **Sunnybunch**
  - Blue flower brush
- **Tassles**
  - Periwinkle flower brush

1988-1989 Year 7

# Newborn Ponies

Though we had met the Newborn Ponies before, this is the first year that they were sold individually rather than as twins. They have the same smaller bodies of the Newborn Twins. Each Newborn Pony was packaged individually on a bubble card with a duck comb and white baby bottle.

$5 to $10

- **Dangles**
  - White baby bottle
  - Gold duck comb

- **Shaggy**
  - White baby bottle
  - Dark pinkish-purple duck comb (**Variation**: yellow duck comb)

$5 to $10

$5 to $10

- **Squirmy**
  - White baby bottle
  - Purple duck comb

- **Tappy**
  - White baby bottle
  - Blue duck comb

$5 to $10

$5 to $10

- **Wiggles**
  - White baby bottle
  - Pink duck comb

- **Yo-Yo**
  - White baby bottle
  - Pale yellow duck comb

$5 to $10

# Perfume Puff Ponies

Perfume Puff Ponies had manes and tails of a very different style than any other set with a soft and puffy texture that was designed to look like a large soft powder puff. Each pony was scented like perfume. Each Perfume Puff Pony came packaged in a box with a flower pick, barrette, and ribbon.

$10 to $15

- **Dainty Dahlia**
    - Yellow flower pick
    - Purple flower barrette
    - Pink ribbon

$10 to $15

- **Daisy Sweet**
    - Pink flower pick
    - Blue flower barrette
    - Purple ribbon

$10 to $15

- **Lavender Lace**
    - Mint flower pick
    - Yellow flower barrette
    - Light purple ribbon

$15 to $20

- **Red Roses**
    - Purple flower pick
    - Aqua bird and lily barrette
    - White ribbon

1988-1989 Year 7

- ❑ **Sweet Lily**
  - ❑ Blue flower pick
  - ❑ Yellow bird and flowers barrette
  - ❑ Pink ribbon

- ❑ **Sweet Suds**
  - ❑ Purple bird and flower barrette
  - ❑ Aqua flower pick
  - ❑ Dark yellow ribbon

## Playtime Baby Brother Ponies

Like the Big Brother Ponies before them, Playtime Baby Brother Ponies had Clydesdale-like hooves and bandanas around their necks. Though baby boy ponies had appeared in the Peek-A-Boo Pony set, this was the first and only set that was comprised solely of little boy ponies. Playtime Brother Ponies had similar head joints to the Peek-A-Boo Ponies that allowed for the heads to turn freely from side to side. Each Playtime Brother Pony was packaged in a box with a stripped bandana, baby dish and spoon, xylophone with mallet, a racecar comb or dog brush, and a ribbon. Baby Leaper is particularly popular with collectors and is usually worth the most from this set.

- ❑ **Baby Countdown**
  - ❑ Blue striped bandana
  - ❑ Green/pink xylophone
  - ❑ Blue mallet
  - ❑ Periwinkle dish
  - ❑ Yellow spoon
  - ❑ Purple dog comb
  - ❑ Pink ribbon

- **Baby Drummer**
  - Red striped bandana
  - Yellow/orange xylophone
  - Dark aqua mallet
  - Dark yellow dish
  - Aqua spoon
  - Red racecar comb
  - Yellow ribbon

- **Baby Leaper**
  - Light pink striped bandana
  - Blue/purple-pink xylophone
  - Greenish yellow mallet
  - Yellow dish
  - Pink spoon
  - Magenta race car comb
  - Yellow ribbon

- **Baby Paws**
  - Yellow striped bandana
  - Blue/purple xylophone
  - Orange mallet
  - Pinkish purple dish
  - Dark pink spoon
  - Orange racecar comb
  - Dark pink ribbon

- **Baby Racer**
  - Aqua striped bandana
  - Yellow/aqua xylophone
  - Blue mallet
  - Light mint green dish
  - Dark yellow spoon
  - Blue dog brush
  - Orange ribbon

1988-1989 Year 7

$10 to $15

- ❏ **Baby Waddles**
    - ❏ Green striped bandana
    - ❏ Aqua/orange xylophone
    - ❏ Orange mallet
    - ❏ Pink dish
    - ❏ Blue spoon
    - ❏ Bright pink ribbon
    - ❏ Dark aqua dog brush

## Princess Brush 'n Grow Ponies

The Princess Brush 'n Grow Ponies were a combination of two great sets of the past. They were princesses, though instead of a raised jeweled symbol on their rump, their symbols were painted on and they had a single raised jewel on their forehead. They did not come with crowns, only barrettes. In addition to being royalty, these ponies also had the hair growth feature of the Brush 'n Grow Ponies. When you gave their tail a tug, it expanded to three times its length. When you then cranked the ponies head back and forth and it would wind back to its shorter length. Each Princess Brush 'n Grow Pony came packaged in a box.

$10 to $15

$10 to $15

- ❏ **Brilliant Bloom**
    - ❏ Peach "I Luv You" barrette
    - ❏ Light purple "I Luv You" barrette
    - ❏ White ribbon
    - ❏ Yellow long hearts and dots brush
    - ❏ Mint green long dots and hearts comb

- ❏ **Glittering Gem**
    - ❏ Pale blue "I Luv You" barrette
    - ❏ Pink "I Luv You" barrette
    - ❏ White ribbon
    - ❏ Light purple long dots and hearts brush
    - ❏ Yellow long hearts and dots comb

- ❏ **Skylark**
    - ❏ Pale yellow "I Luv You" barrette
    - ❏ Medium pink "I Luv You" barrette
    - ❏ White ribbon
    - ❏ Pink long dots and hearts brush
    - ❏ Periwinkle long dots and hearts comb

- ❏ **Star Gleamer**
    - ❏ Pale aqua "I Luv You" barrette
    - ❏ Pale pink "I Luv You" barrette
    - ❏ White ribbon
    - ❏ Aqua long hearts and dots brush
    - ❏ Purple long hearts and dots comb

## Sparkle Ponies

The Sparkle Ponies had translucent glittery bodies and tinsel in their manes and tails. This set was particularly interesting because these same ponies were released twice. The version on this page was sold in stores and a second set was available only through mail order offer. The key difference between the store and mail order sets, aside from a change in hair color for some, was that the store bought set did not have a second smaller symbol on each pony's check while the mail order versions did. Sparkle Ponies all had symbols that were outer space-themed. Each Sparkle Pony was packaged on a bubble card with a brush or comb.

- ❏ **Napper**
    - ❏ Purple moon comb

- ❏ **Sky Rocket**
    - ❏ Pink shooting star brush

1988-1989 Year 7

- **Star Dancer**
  - Yellow shooting star comb

- **Star Hopper**
  - Dark pink shooting star brush

- **Sunspot**
  - Orange sun pick

- **Twinkler**
  - Blue crescent moon comb

# Sunshine Ponies

This tropical set of ponies was ready for fun in the sun! Sunshine Ponies had a streak of hair that, when exposed to sunlight, would change color. Once back in the shade, however, it would revert back to its more subdued original color. Sadly, the color changing streak in the Sunshine Ponies' hair had a tendency to get dry and frizzy over time.

Each Sunshine Pony was packaged with either a butterfly brush or a sun comb on a bubble card.

At right, Beachball after sun exposure.

103

The My Little Pony G1 Collector's Inventory

$5 to $10

- **Beachball**
  - Purple sun pick

$5 to $10

- **Mainsail**
  - Light green butterfly brush

$5 to $10

- **Sand Digger**
  - Pink butterfly brush

$5 to $10

- **Seaflower**
  - Yellow sun pick

$5 to $10

- **Shoreline**
  - Sea green butterfly brush

$5 to $10

- **Wave Runner**
  - Blue sun pick

1988-1989 Year 7

# Sweetheart Sister Ponies

The Sweetheart Sister Ponies introduced an entirely new pony body type which was used in many later sets. With thinner bodies and long legs, the Sweetheart Sister Ponies (commonly abbreviated SHS) were designed to be young adult or teenage ponies. All the ponies in this set had painted eye shadow and each came with an earring of a flower with a twisted stem. This earring, though not molded, was plastic and impossible to remove without breaking. The stems on the earrings very often cracked off so an intact earring is important to getting the best price for a SHS pony. They also came with a wide lace-like ribbon instead of the traditional ribbon.

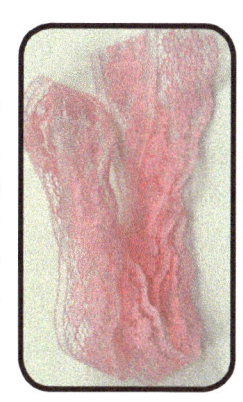

- **Dainty**
    - Purple irremovable earring
    - Purple lace ribbon
    - Purple flower brush

- **Fancy Flower**
    - Peach irremovable earring
    - Peach lace ribbon
    - Peach butterfly brush

- **Flowerburst**
    - Pink irremovable earring
    - Purple lace ribbon
    - Pink flower brush

105

- ❏ **Frilly Flower**
    - ❏ Pink irremovable earring
    - ❏ Pink lace ribbon
    - ❏ Pink butterfly brush

- ❏ **Spring Song**
    - ❏ Yellow irremovable earring
    - ❏ Yellow lace ribbon
    - ❏ Yellow butterfly brush

- ❏ **Wild Flower**
    - ❏ Aqua irremovable earring
    - ❏ Aqua lace ribbon
    - ❏ Aqua flower brush

# Windy Wing Ponies

The Windy Wing Ponies were essentially the Summer Wing Ponies, reincarnated. They had nearly identical wing structures and setting to the Summer Wing Ponies. The Windy Wing Ponies all had sky themed symbols. Windy Wing Ponies also each had a small symbol on either their cheek or forehead. Each Windy Wing Pony was packaged in a box with a sun pick.

1988-1989 Year 7

$35 to $40

- Cool Breeze
  - Blue sun pick

$15 to $20

- Flurry
  - Green sun pick

$15 to $20

- Moon Jumper
  - Pink sun pick

$15 to $20

- Starry Wings
  - Dark green sun pick

$15 to $20

- Sun Glider
  - Yellow sun pick

$15 to $20

- Whirly
  - Orange sun pick

# 1989-1990
## Year 8

Year 8 introduced several new themes including Prom Queen and Glittery Sweetheart Sisters, Baby Sparkle Ponies, Rainbow Curl Ponies, Tropical Ponies, and Sweetsteps Ballerina Ponies. A very unique set of Drink 'n Wet Ponies could do just as their name suggests: drink water and wet their diapers. Year 8 was also the year that ponies both shrunk and grew into the tiny Petite Pony and larger Dream Beauty toy lines. The traditional set size of six ponies was reduced to four ponies in most cases this year.

The My Little Pony G1 Collector's Inventory

# Baby Sparkle Ponies

Though the Baby Sparkle Ponies had the same translucent bodies as the adult set, they did not have tinsel in their hair, nor were they the children of that set. Some were, oddly enough, named after ponies from the first 2 years of MLP, though they looked nothing like their namesakes.

- **Baby Firefly**
  - Light blue shooting stars comb

- **Baby Gusty**
  - Pink shooting stars comb

- **Baby North Star**
  - Light pinkish purple shooting star brush

- **Baby Starflower**
  - Dark aqua shooting star brush

# The Christmas Pony

Merry Treat was the only Holiday pony ever offered in stores (though others were offered in mail offers).

- **Merry Treat**
  - Yellow ribbon
  - Green Christmas tree comb

1989-1990 Year 8

# Baby Drink 'n Wet Ponies

Like a classic baby doll, Baby Drink 'n Wet Ponies came with a bottle that you could fill with water and have them drink. As they drank the water, it would cause hearts to appear on their diapers once wet.

Prices below are for mint condition, loose, Baby Drink 'n Wet Ponies. Ponies from this set that are complete with accessories can increase in value by $10 or more.

$5 to $10

- ❑ **Baby Cuddles**
- ❑ Purple BABY changing table
- ❑ Purple ribbon
- ❑ Purple magic diaper
- ❑ Green magic diaper
- ❑ Magic diaper box
- ❑ Dark aqua duck comb
- ❑ Pinkish purple squeeze bottle

- ❑ **Baby Flicker**
- ❑ Blue BABY changing table
- ❑ Greenish blue ribbon
- ❑ Purple magic diaper
- ❑ Green magic diaper
- ❑ Magic diaper box
- ❑ White duck comb
- ❑ Aqua squeeze bottle

$5 to $10

- ❑ **Baby Rainfeather**
- ❑ Yellow BABY changing table
- ❑ Hot pink ribbon
- ❑ Purple magic diaper
- ❑ Green magic diaper
- ❑ Magic diaper box
- ❑ Purple duck comb
- ❑ Purple squeeze bottle

- ❑ **Baby Snookums**
- ❑ Aqua BABY changing table
- ❑ Dark pink ribbon (**Variation**: gold ribbon)
- ❑ Purple magic diaper
- ❑ Green magic diaper
- ❑ Magic diaper box
- ❑ Pink duck comb
- ❑ Pink squeeze bottle

$5 to $10

$5 to $10

# Glitter Sweetheart Sister Ponies

The Glitter Sweetheart Sister Ponies, like the previous set of SHS ponies, had thin bodies and an irremovable earring in one ear. They had glittery symbols all over their sides. The strangest part of this set, however, was that some of the ponies names seem, to have been mixed up as not all names match the symbols.

- **Bright Night**
  - Blue irremovable earring
  - Dark purple glittery stars pick

- **Starflash**
  - Pink irremovable earring
  - Red glittery stars pick

- **Sunblossom**
  - Purple irremovable earring
  - Blue glittery stars pick

- **Twinkler**
  - Pink irremovable earring
  - Orange glittery stars pick

1989-1990 Year 8

# Pony Bride

The Pony Bride was an all white pony that came with tinsel in her hair and many accessories for her wedding. She was unnamed. The bride ponies are often sought out for use as wedding cake toppers.

- ❏ **Pony Bride**
    - ❏ Lace veil
    - ❏ Diamond ring
    - ❏ Wedding cake
    - ❏ Pink flower pick
    - ❏ Blue ribbon

$5 to $10

# Prom Queen Sweetheart Sister Ponies

Like other Sweetheart Sister sets before them, the Prom Queen Sweetheart Sister Ponies had eye shadow and an earring. However, they also each came with perfume and a ruffle that was also a scrunchie for you to wear in your hair.

- ❏ **Cha Cha**
    - ❏ Light pink/silver ruffle
    - ❏ Purple flower barrette
    - ❏ Orange glittery star pick
    - ❏ Bottle of Prom Sweetheart perfume
    - ❏ Salmon irremovable earring

- ❏ **Daisy Dancer**
    - ❏ Blue/silver ruffle
    - ❏ Yellow flower barrette
    - ❏ Blue glittery star pick
    - ❏ Bottle of Prom Sweetheart perfume
    - ❏ Pink irremovable earring

- ❏ **Pretty Belle**
    - ❏ Yellow/silver ruffle
    - ❏ Aqua flower barrette
    - ❏ Gold glittery star pick
    - ❏ Bottle of Prom Sweetheart perfume
    - ❏ Purple irremovable earring

- ❏ **Sweet Sundrop**
    - ❏ Pink/silver ruffle
    - ❏ Aqua flower barrette
    - ❏ Magenta glittery star pick
    - ❏ Bottle of Prom Sweetheart perfume
    - ❏ Blue irremovable earring

1989-1990 Year 8

# Rainbow Curl Ponies

Like the Rainbow Ponies of the second year of MLP, the Rainbow Curl Ponies had four colors in their mane and tail. However, instead of having straight hair, their hair came in tight ringlet curls (like the hair of the Candy Cane Ponies) with each curl comprised one of one. Rainbow Curl Ponies had their symbols all the way up the sides of their bodies.

$5 to $10

$5 to $10

❑ **Raincurl**
   ❑ Purple shooting star brush
   ❑ Yellow ribbon

❑ **Ringlet**
   ❑ Pink shooting star brush
   ❑ Orange ribbon

$5 to $10

$5 to $10

❑ **Streaky**
   ❑ Blue shooting star brush
   ❑ Pink ribbon

❑ **Stripes**
   ❑ Yellow shooting star brush
   ❑ Purple ribbon

# Sweetsteps Ballerina Ponies

The Sweetsteps Ballerina Ponies were the first ponies who were pose-able. With moveable heads and legs, they could be posed in a variety of ways. Their symbols were on their leotards instead of on their rumps and each pony came with a tutu.

$5 to $10

- **Posey Rose**
- Aqua ribbon
- Light green opaque stars pick
- Lavender flower barrette
- Yellow flower barrette
- Pink tutu

- **Silky Slipper**
- White ribbon
- Pink/purple (lighter) opaque star pick
- Light aqua flower barrette
- Pink flower barrette
- Magenta tutu

$5 to $10

$5 to $10

- **Tip Toes**
- Bright pink ribbon
- Pink/purple (darker) opaque star pick
- Blue flower barrette
- Pink flower barrette
- Yellow tutu

- **Twinkle Dancer**
- Yellow ribbon
- Orange opaque 3-stars pick
- White flower barrette
- Peach flower barrette
- Purple tutu

$5 to $10

1989-1990 Year 8

# Tropical Ponies

The Tropical Ponies had wild neon colors for their body and mane. Each pony's eye was lined with eye shadow and each came with only a brush. Each pony in this set shares a name with a Tropical Fairy Tail Bird, another Hasbro toy.

$5 to $10

❑ **Hula Hula**
  ❑ Yellow bird brush

$5 to $10

❑ **Piña Colada**
  ❑ Blue fish comb

$5 to $10

❑ **Sea Breeze**
  ❑ Hot pink bird brush

$5 to $10

❑ **Tootie Tails**
  ❑ Magenta fish comb

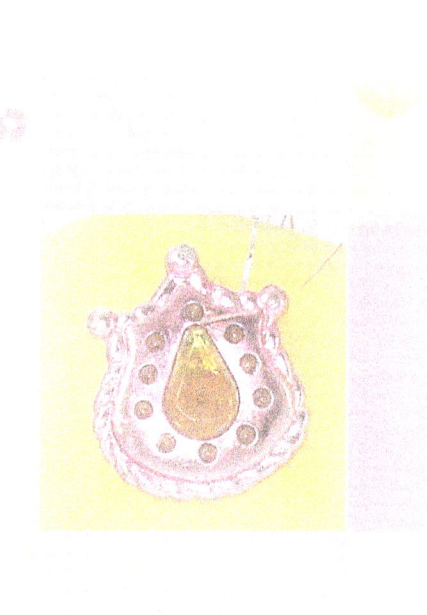

# 1990-1991
## Year 9

Seemingly all of the ponies released in Year 9 had a unique gimmick associated with them. Ponies could no longer just stand and be pretty, they had to glow in the dark (Glow 'n Show), hide secret treasures (Secret Surprise), have 3-D pockets (Precious Pockets), or be extra tiny (Teeny Tiny Ponies). Petite Ponies continued into its second year and new My Little Puppy, Kitty, and Bunny Families were introduced in sets called Li'l Litters.

# Baby Ballerina Ponies

Like the adult Sweetsteps Ballerina Ponies, the Baby Ballerina Ponies were completely pose-able, though they did not have symbols on their back or come with tutus.

$5 to $10

- **Baby Softsteps**
  - Purple flower brush

$5 to $10

- **Baby Sweetsteps**
  - Blue flower brush

$5 to $10

- **Baby Tippytoes**
  - Yellow flower brush

$5 to $10

- **Baby Toe Dancer**
  - Dark pink flower brush

1990-1991 Year 9

# Baby Rainbow Ponies

Though Rainbow Ponies had been introduced as early as the second year of MLP, this was the first year there were Baby Rainbow Ponies. Though not the children of any previous Rainbow Pony, the Baby Rainbow Ponies had multi-colored manes like the adults before them.

$10 to $15

❑ **Baby Brightbow**
 ❑ Blue flower brush

$10 to $15

❑ **Baby Rainribbon**
 ❑ Yellow flower brush

$10 to $15

❑ **Baby Starbow**
 ❑ Dark pink flower brush

$10 to $15

❑ **Baby Sunribbon**
 ❑ Coral flower brush

# Firefly's Adventure

Firefly, one of the most popular of the original ponies, returned this year in a special edition. Repackaged with the very first My Little Pony TV special on a VHS cassette, *Rescue from Midnight Castle*, renamed as *Firefly's Adventure*, this version of Firefly was in a completely different pose with darker colors than the original release. **Collector's Note:** The VHS version of *Firefly's Adventure* packaged with this set is highly sought after as it is the full special. As of print time, there has yet to be a DVD release of this special that was unedited.

- **Firefly (Collector's Edition)**
  - Firefly's Adventure VHS (previously titled *Rescue from Midnight Castle*)
  - Purple flower brush

## Glow 'n Show Ponies

The Glow 'n Show Ponies had translucent bodies like the Sparkle Ponies, only, instead of being filled with sparkles, they were filled with tiny hearts and stars that glowed in the dark. The distribution of the items inside the ponies was random so no two Glow 'n Show Ponies are exactly alike. A alternant version of Dazzleglow with blue hearts was also available. The Glow 'n Show Ponies were featured in an episode of the *My Little Pony Tales* cartoon series.

- **Brightglow**
  - Green butterfly brush

- **Dazzleglow**
  - Hot pink butterfly brush

1990-1991 Year 9

- **Happyglow**
  - Yellow butterfly brush

- **Starglow**
  - Bright orange butterfly brush

- **Dazzleglow** (blue hearts version)
  - Hot pink butterfly brush

## Precious Pocket Ponies

Precious Pocket Ponies had 3-D symbols that formed a pocket on one side of their body. A silver cord attached a small accessory to the pony. This attached accessory, which was related to the pony's symbol, could be placed inside the pony's pocket. Each Precious Pocket Pony was packaged on a bubble card with a flower brush.

- **Bubblefish**
  - Blue flower brush

- **Bunny Hop**
  - Light blue flower brush

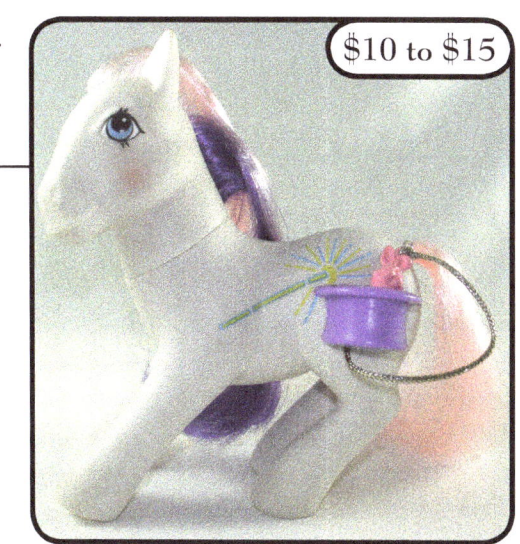

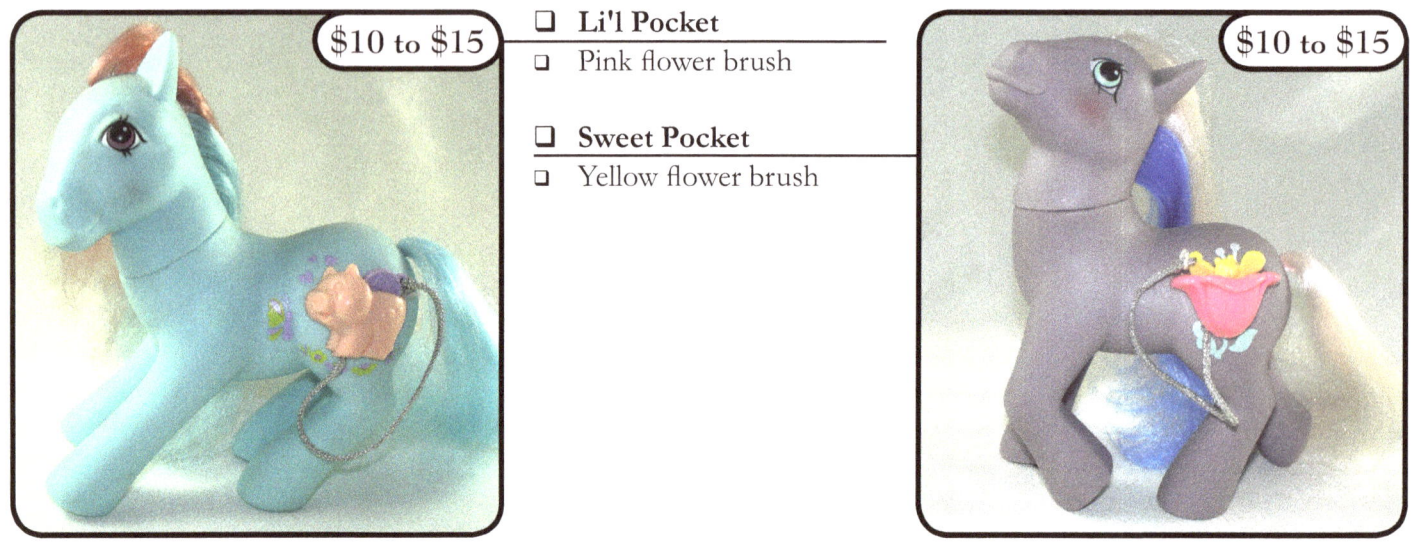

- **Li'l Pocket**
  - Pink flower brush

- **Sweet Pocket**
  - Yellow flower brush

# Pretty Ponies

Pretty Ponies were similar to Sweetheart Sister Ponies but simplified in design as they were meant to be a girl's first pony (even though MLP was in its second to last year). They did not come with earrings as previous Sweetheart Sister ponies did and were all solid colors.

- **Beautybloom**
  - Blue standard comb

- **Flower Dream**
  - Red standard comb

- **Gardenglow**
  - Dark pink standard comb

- **Rosy Love**
  - Blue-green standard comb

1990-1991 Year 9

# Princess Ponies
**(third set)**

This was the third set of Princess Ponies (fourth if we include the Princess Brush 'n Grow Ponies). Both ponies were in the same pose and had long eyelashes. These ponies were not given official names but both have royalty themed symbols.

❑ **(pink body)**
❑ Hot pink collar and cape
❑ Periwinkle blue frog brush
❑ sliver crown

❑ **(purple body)**
❑ Aqua collar and cape
❑ Dark pink frog brush
❑ Sliver crown

# Rockin' Beat Ponies

The Rockin' Beat Ponies were a wild bunch of rock stars with vibrant neon colors, crimped hair (in homage to the 80's when so called "hair bands" were very popular), heavy eye shadow and neon guitars that doubled as brushes. These ponies also made an appearance in the *My Little Pony Tales* cartoon series.

The My Little Pony G1 Collector's Inventory

- **Half Note**
  - Neon green guitar brush with strap
- **Pretty Beat**
  - Yellow guitar brush with strap

- **Sweet Notes**
  - Orange guitar brush with strap
- **Tuneful**
  - Hot pink guitar brush with strap

## Secret Surprise Ponies

Secret Surprise Ponies had colorful decorative capes on their backs instead of symbols. These plastic capes were actually the cover of a secret compartment that snapped opened when you put their key into the broach on the pony's neck. Inside the compartment was a surprise for you (play jewelry) and a little hiding place for various treasures. Because of this hiding place, Secret Surprise Ponies are a little larger than normal ponies.

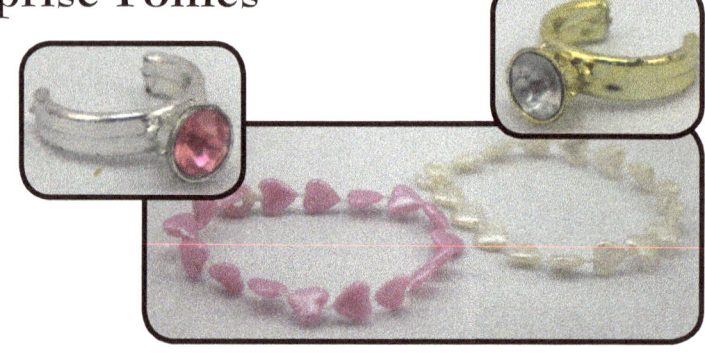

1990-1991 Year 9

$10 to $15

- **Pretty Puff**
    - Peach bow and pony cameo comb
    - Pink key
    - Gold ring with clear jewel

$10 to $15

- **Secret Beauty**
    - Mint green bow and pony cameo comb
    - Purple key
    - Silver ring with pink gem

$10 to $15

- **Secret Star**
    - Pink bow and pony cameo comb
    - Aqua key
    - White beaded heart bracelet

$10 to $15

- **Stardazzle**
    - Purple bow and pony cameo comb
    - Peach key
    - Purple beaded heart bracelet

# Teeny Tiny Ponies

The Teeny Tiny Ponies were meant to be even younger than the Newborn Ponies and they were even smaller with tiny, thin feline-like faces.

- **Little Giggles**
  - Peach duck comb

- **Little Honey Pie**
  - Yellow teddy bear brush

- **Little Tabby**
  - Purple duck comb

- **Little Whiskers**
  - Mint green teddy bear brush

# 1991-1992
## Year 10

As a decade of My Little Pony came to a close, Year 10 marked the end of the first generation (G1) of My Little Pony in the United States as Hasbro changed the My Little Pony packaging to bright pink boxes celebrating the 10th anniversary of the toys. Unique pony sets celebrated the occasion including the Birthday Pony, Fancy Mermaid Ponies, Colorswirl Ponies, Sweet Kisses Ponies, Sippin' Soda Ponies and Teeny Pony Twins ponies to name a few. This year also gave collectors the first talking ponies.

# Birthday Pony

The Birthday Pony was a colorful explosion of shapes and streamers with curling ribbon in her hair and a special surprise for you in a wrapped present. While you could use her to celebrate your birthday, she was made to celebrate the 10th birthday of My Little Pony as Hasbro celebrated the one decade anniversary since the original set of MLP was available in stores.

❑ **Birthday Pony**
   ❑ Gift box
   ❑ Surprise gift (metallic heart necklace)
   ❑ Yellow shooting stars comb

$10 to $15

# Bridal Beauty

Bridal Beauty was essentially a re-issue of Pony Bride as she was in the identical pose, though with a different symbol.

❑ **Bridal Beauty**
   ❑ 2-layer veil with pink beaded headband
   ❑ Silver wedding ring
   ❑ Pink bouquet/barrette
   ❑ Purple flower brush

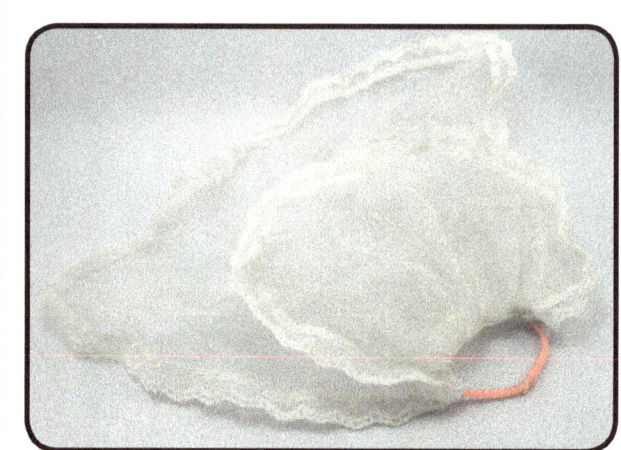

$5 to $10

1991-1992 Year 10

# Colorswirl Ponies

In addition to the standard symbol design, Colorswirl Ponies also had large, colored, zebra-like stripes all over their bodies. They were all in the same pose as the Pony Bride.

$20 to $25

❏ **Lovebeam**
   ❏ Neon blue shooting star comb

$20 to $25

❏ **Springy**
   ❏ Green shooting star comb

$20 to $25

❏ **Starswirl**
   ❏ Orange shooting star comb

131

# Fancy Mermaid Ponies

Fancy Mermaid Ponies were possibly the strangest set of MLP ever. Unlike Sea Ponies, which looked like sea horses, Fancy Mermaid Ponies were regular ponies from the midsection up, but had a pearlized mermaid tail. Their faces were similar to Teeny Tiny Ponies. Each pony also had an identifying symbol on her chest.

- **Baby Pearly**
  - Neon blue fish comb

- **Baby Sea Princess**
  - Hot pink fish comb

- **Baby Sea Shimmer**
  - Orange fish comb

1991-1992 Year 10

# Flower Fantasy Ponies

Flower Fantasy Ponies had flower and ribbon symbols all over their bodies and faces.

$15 to $20

❑ **Flowerbelle**
  ❑ Mint green flower brush

$15 to $20

❑ **Love Petal**
  ❑ Dark pink flower brush

$15 to $20

❑ **Sweet Blossom**
  ❑ Light yellow flower brush

# Paradise Baby Ponies

Though not named as such, the Paradise Baby Ponies were essentially Baby Tropical Ponies with their wild neon colors and tropical theme.

$15 to $20

- ❑ **Baby Beach Ball**
    - ❑ Blue flower brush

$15 to $20

- ❑ **Baby Palm Tree**
    - ❑ Dark purple flower brush

$15 to $20

- ❑ **Baby Pineapple**
    - ❑ Hot pink flower brush

1991-1992 Year 10

# Soda Sippin' Ponies

Soda Sippin' Ponies were scented like their flavor of choice and had tight ringlet curls like the Rainbow Curl and Candy Cane Ponies before them. They also had a large hole in their muzzle that allowed the straw on their ice cream sundae to fit into their mouths. By squeezing the sundae or pony, the "bubbles" (rainbow foam beads) in the straw would go up and down, making it seem like the pony was drinking.

$10 to $15

- **Chocolate Delight**
  - Aqua lollipop brush
  - Chocolate ice cream float with drinking straw

- **Strawberry Scoops**
  - Pink lollipop brush
  - Strawberry ice cream float with drinking straw

$10 to $15

135

# Sundazzle Ponies

Like the Sunshine Ponies before them, the Sundazzle Ponies had manes that changed color in the sun. Unlike the other set, however, Sundazzle Ponies were in the Sweetheart Sister pony style and had neon body colors with crimped hair.

$5 to $10

- ❏ **Sunbeam**
    - ❏ Neon blue sun pick

$5 to $10

- ❏ **Sunglory**
    - ❏ Hot pink sun pick

$5 to $10

- ❏ **Sunsplasher**
    - ❏ Purple sun pick

Sunbeam, after sun exposure

1991-1992 Year 10

# Sweet Kisses Ponies

The Sweet Kisses Ponies came with a lipstick tube where the lipstick itself was a small red sponge. When you dabbed the sponge in cold water and applied it to your pony, lipstick would appear on your pony's lips. When you gave her a kiss, the heat of the kiss would make the lipstick disappear again. The Sweet Kisses Ponies were Sweetheart Sister-style ponies, without earrings and with tinsel in their hair. Over time, their lips may lose the ability to change color.

❑ **Happy Hugs**
　❑ Purple lipstick tube

❑ **Lovin' Kisses**
　❑ Blue lipstick tube

❑ **Ruby Lips**
　❑ Yellow lipstick tube

# Teeny Pony Twins

The Teeny Tiny Ponies returned in the final year in sets of twins. Each pair was nearly identical with a tiny little difference for you to find. Unlike past sets of twins, however, these twins came with either the number 1 or 2 on the underside of their foot to help you tell them apart.

$5 to $10 each

- ❑ Bootsie
- ❑ Tootsie
    - ❑ Pink tiny baby bottle
    - ❑ Blue tiny baby bottle

**Telling your twins apart:** While both have booties as their symbol, Tootsie's have turquoise trim while Bootsie's do not. They both have a tiny bootie on their body, though it is on Tootsie's cheek and Bootsie's left front leg. Bootsie is numbered 1 while Tootsie is 2.

$5 to $10 each

- ❑ Rattles
- ❑ Tattles
    - ❑ Yellow BABY necklace with yellow text
    - ❑ Purple BABY necklace with purple text

**Telling your twins apart:** The rattle on Tattles' symbol has a hole through the center of the handle while the rattle on Rattles has a solid handle. They both also have a tiny pink bow on their bodies though Rattles has it above her left eye while Tattles has it on her right hind leg. Rattles is numbered 1 while Tattles is numbered 2.

1991-1992 Year 10

$5 to $10 each

- Sniffles
- Snookums
    - Purple dish
    - Two coral spoons

**Telling your twins apart:** Snookums' symbol is a flower with leaves on its stem while Sniffles' symbol does not have leaves. Snookums also has small purple dots on her right hind leg, while Sniffles has them on her cheek. Sniffles is numbered 1 while Snookums is 2.

## Sweet Talkin' Ponies

My Little Pony was finally given a voice with the set of Sweet Talkin' Ponies. Their sayings rotated through three sayings, with "I love you" as every other one. The sayings were "I love you," "Comb my hair," and "I'm pretty." Though the Sweet Talkin' Ponies were unnamed in the US, they did have names in the UK. The names listed below are the names of the UK ponies of the same set which were identical in appearence.

$5 to $10

$5 to $10

- pink body (Chatterbox)
    - Purple long dots and hearts comb

- purple (Talk-A-Lot)
    - Pinkish purple long dots and hearts comb

139

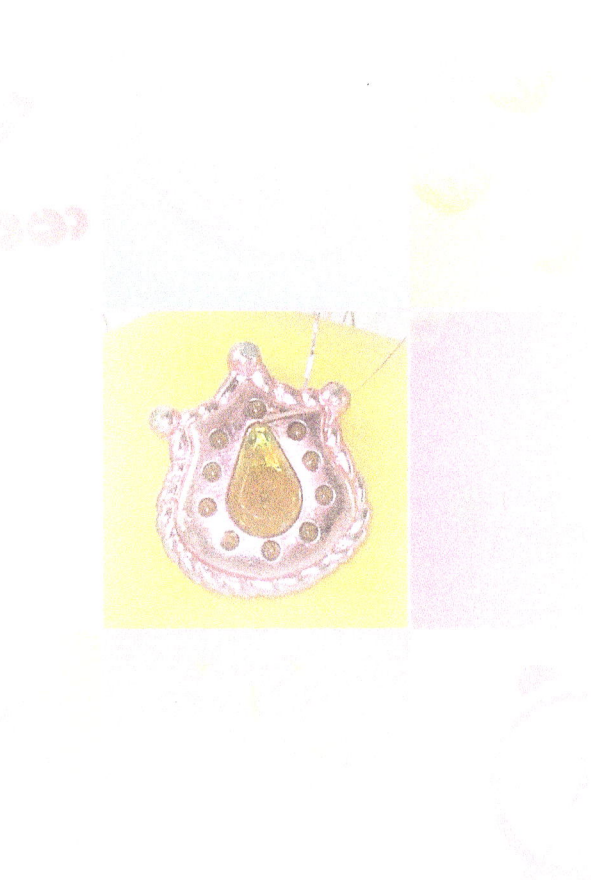

# Petite Ponies

Available from 1989 to 1991, Petite Ponies were miniature My Little Ponies that stood just a little over an inch high. With a special horseshoe indentation on their bases that worked like a key, they could unlock special features of their tiny playsets. Petite Ponies could be purchased in several different sets. Aside from the Petite Ponies who were packaged with playsets, they were not given names and are identified by their body color, hair color, and symbol. All Petite Ponies were either earth ponies or pegasus as no unicorns were made.

# Pony Parade

The first set of Petite Ponies ever released, the Pony Parade ponies, all had molded manes and tails.

- ❑ Green with yellow hair and purple crayon (pegasus)
- ❑ Lavender with orange hair and purple ballet slippers
- ❑ Dark pink with yellow hair and white swan
- ❑ Blue with pink hair and purple teddy bear
- ❑ White with pink hair and purple ice cream cone (pegasus)
- ❑ Orange with purple hair and aqua teapot
- ❑ Blue with orange hair and purple umbrella
- ❑ Pink with yellow hair and aqua butterfly
- ❑ Dark pink with aqua hair and white beach ball
- ❑ Yellow with aqua hair and orange sun

$1 to $5 each

# Sparkle Ponies

Sparkle Ponies had translucent bodies, but unlike the later Twinkle Ponies set, they had molded tails and did not have glitter in their bodies.

- ❑ Melon with yellow hair and yellow ring
- ❑ Purple with pink hair and yellow perfume bottle
- ❑ Green with orange hair and purple balloons (pegasus)
- ❑ Blue with pink hair and ice cream soda
- ❑ Orange with purple hair and red hot air balloon

Petite Ponies

$1 to $5 each

## Pretty 'n Pearly

The Pretty 'n Pearly Petites had a pearly glaze covering their bodies and molded manes and tails.

- Yellow with pink hair and aqua leaf
- Purple with pink hair and pink umbrella
- Pink with blue hair and blue heart with wings
- Aqua blue with yellow hair and purple moon with nightcap
- Orange with purple hair and blue seashell

$5 to $10 each

# Ponytail Petites

The Petites in the Ponytail sets are generally the most common sets of petites. Instead of having the molded tails like the previous sets, they had brushable tails. Theses petites were sold in three different sets with each set having four ponies. Each pony in a set had one of the following symbols: clock, mirror, pizza, or hairbrush. Each set also came packaged with a small star pick.

$1 to $5 each

### Set A
- Light blue earth pony with yellow hair, white bow, pink-purple mirror symbol
- White earth pony with pink hair, lavender bow, light green brush and comb symbol
- Gold earth pony with purple hair, pink bow, aqua clock symbol
- Pink pegasus with dark pink hair, yellow bow, light orange pizza symbol
    - Dark pink single star pick

### Set B
- Purple earth pony with yellow hair, aqua bow, gold mirror symbol
- Pink earth pony with aqua hair, lavender bow, purple brush and comb symbol
- Blue earth pony with dark pink hair, yellow bow, orange clock symbol
- Yellow pegasus with blue hair, pink bow, pink pizza symbol
    - Orange single star pick

Petite Ponies

### Set C
- ☐ Yellow earth pony with white hair, blue bow, red-orange mirror symbol
- ☐ Aqua earth pony with pink hair, yellow bow, yellow brush and comb symbol
- ☐ Dark pink earth pony with yellow hair, aqua bow, blue clock symbol
- ☐ Bright orange pegasus with aqua hair, pink bow, pink pizza symbol
    - ☐ Blue orange star pick

## Twinkle Ponies

These Petites had translucent bodies with glitter and brushable tails. Also sold in three sets of four, though unnamed, their sets are usually distinguished amongst collectors by the theme of the symbols.

$5 to $10 each

### Set A (Party Themed Set)
- ☐ Dark pink earth pony with blue hair, blue cupcake symbol
- ☐ Dark blue earth pony with peach hair, peach party favor symbol
- ☐ Pale pink earth pony with lime green hair, light blue present symbol
- ☐ Aqua pegasus with dark pink hair, light green party hat symbol
    - ☐ Dark purple single star pick

### Set B (Royalty Themed Set)

- ❑ Pale orange earth pony with pink-purple hair, aqua tower symbol
- ❑ Pale pink earth pony with aqua hair, green treasure chest symbol
- ❑ Yellow earth pony with pink hair, blue wand symbol
- ❑ Pale pink pegasus with yellow hair, yellow crown symbol
    - ❑ Hot pink single star pick

### Set C (Music Themed Set)

- ❑ Dark purple earth pony with pink hair, pink radio symbol
- ❑ Pale pink pegasus with lime green hair, yellow records symbol
- ❑ Light blue earth pony with dark pink mane and red tail, peach saxophone symbol
- ❑ Orange earth pony with purple hair, pink guitar symbol
    - ❑ Yellow single star pick

# Bright Sight

Each Petite in this set had a tropical or beach themed symbol and, like their set name suggests, their bodies and hair were brightly colored. As with each of the sets from this year, though unnamed, the sets had a theme to their symbols that collectors often use to identify them by.

$5 to $10 each

# Petite Ponies

### Set A (Fruit Themed Set)

- ❏ Dark pink earth pony with dark red-orange mane and orange tail, purple grapes symbol
- ❏ Yellow earth pony with pink-purple mane and dark pink tail, red-orange watermelon slice symbol
- ❏ Light blue pegasus with dark pink mane and red tail, yellow pineapple symbol
- ❏ Peach earth pony with blue hair, dark pink cherries symbol
    - ❏ Orange single star pick

### Set B (Transportation Themed Set)

- ❏ Dark pink earth pony with blue hair, light orange skateboard symbol
- ❏ Dark pink with yellow mane and neon yellow tail, blue scooter symbol
- ❏ Gold earth pony with blue hair, dark pink bike symbol
- ❏ Bright yellow pegasus with dark pink mane and red tail, red-orange roller skate symbol
    - ❏ Mustard single star pick

### Set C (Summer Themed Set)

- ❏ Dark pink earth pony with yellow hair, purple heart shaped sunglasses symbol
- ❏ Bright yellow earth pony with blue hair, light green framed palmed beach symbol
- ❏ Bright orange pegasus with a dark pink mane and red tail, blue sailboat sailing into sunset symbol
- ❏ Purple earth pony with yellow hair, dark pink cocktail symbol
    - ❏ Green single star pick

## Glowing Magic

A unique feature of Petites in this set is that their bodies would glow in the dark. Unlike with the other sets, Glowing Magic sets are not as well defined in theme with nearly all just having to do with sleeping and night.

$5 to $10 each

The My Little Pony G1 Collector's Inventory

### Set A

- ❑ Aqua earth pony with light pink hair, light pink toothpaste & toothbrush symbol
- ❑ Pale yellow earth pony with blue mane and tail, pink moon with nightcap symbol
- ❑ Pink pegasus with white hair w/white hair, blue candle symbol
- ❑ Gold earth pony with indigo hair, coral shooting stars symbol
    - ❑ Dark pink single star pick

### Set B

- ❑ Purple earth pony with pink hair, aqua gloworm symbol
- ❑ Dark pink earth pony with blue hair, yellow teddy bear symbol
- ❑ Turquoise earth pony with coral hair, purple cradle symbol
- ❑ Pale yellow pegasus with purple hair, coral baby bottle symbol
    - ❑ Yellow single star pick

### Set C

- ❑ Yellow earth pony with pink hair, pink bunny slippers symbol
- ❑ Pale yellow earth pony with dark pink hair, turquoise sheep symbol
- ❑ Purple pegasus with orange hair, aqua clock symbol
- ❑ Coral earth pony with blue hair, purple bed symbol
    - ❑ Purple single star pick

## Petite Pony Homes

Three different house playsets, each with a named Petite Pony, could be added to your Petite collection. All had the same basic building structure, but came in different colors with different accessories and stickers. The interesting thing about each playset is that the accessory colors vary greatly from set to set, even when looking at two of the same house. Prices listed are for houses with all accessories.

- ❑ **Happy Hearts Cottage**
- ❑ **Puddles** is a pink earth pony with molded blue hair and a yellow duck symbol
- ❑ **Puddles (Variation:** brushable tail)
- ❑ 2 fence pieces
- ❑ Bathtub
- ❑ Couch
- ❑ Vanity
- ❑ Seesaw (2 pieces)

$15 to $20

$1 to $5

148

Petite Ponies

$1 to $5

$15 to $20

❑ **Pony Prints Cabin**
❑ **Flurry** is a pink earth pony with molded aqua hair and a yellow mittens symbol.
❑ **Flurry** (**Variation:** brushable tail)
❑   2 fence pieces
❑   Fireplace
❑   Bed
❑   Country bench
❑   Whishing well

$15 to $20

❑ **Whinny Winks Inn**
❑ **Little Flitter** is an orange pegasus with moded lavender hair and a blue candle symbol.
❑ **Little Flitter** (**Variation:** curly tail)
❑   2 fence pieces
❑   Porch swing
❑   Bed
❑   Dresser
❑   Table

$1 to $5

# Petite Pony Shoppes

Consisting of a market, a beauty shop, and an ice cream parlor, these playsets added more places for the Petite Ponies to visit. Like the Homes playsets, the Shoppes also shared the same basic building structure but came in different colors with different accessories and stickers. They also came packaged with a named Petite Pony. The accessories in these sets were also available in many different color combinations. Prices listed are for sets with all accessories. Like the homes, the ponies that came with these sets had two variations.

- **Happy Hoof Market**
- **Tabby** is a dark pink earth pony with molded purple hair and a purple cash register symbol
- **Tabby** (**Variation:** curly tail)
- 2 fence pieces
- Grocery cart
- Scooter
- Grocery bag
- Produce counter
- Freezer
- Gumball machine

- **Mane Delight Beauty Shoppe**
- **Misty** is a yellow earth pony with molded pink hair and a purple perfume bottle symbol
- **Misty** (**Variation:** brushable tail)
- 2 fence pieces
- Hair dryers
- Shampoo bowl
- Jewelry counter
- Mirror
- Table
- Magazine rack

Petite Ponies

- ❑ **Twinkle Treats Ice Cream Shoppe**
- ❑ **Floater** is a lime green earth pony with molded yellow hair and an orange soda bottle symbol
- ❑ **Floater** (**Variation:** brushable tail)
- ❑ 2 fence pieces
- ❑ Menu board
- ❑ Booth
- ❑ Ice cream cart
- ❑ Small table
- ❑ Slide
- ❑ Juke box

## Prancing Pretty Carousel

This playset played music (the awning wound like a music box) and when a Petite Pony activated it with her hoof key, the swing seats turned like a real carousel. In addition to lots of fun themed accessories, this set also came with two Petite ponies. Like the other Petite playsets, the colors of accessories often vary.

The ponies themselves are valued at $5 to $10 each.

- ❑ **Carousel**
- ❑ **Topper** (two ticket symbol)
- ❑ **Whirly** (pinwheel symbol)
- ❑ **Topper** (**Variation:** brushable tail)
- ❑ **Whirly** (**Variation:** brushable tail)
- ❑ Ticket booth
- ❑ Seesaw (2 pieces)
- ❑ Slide
- ❑ Teacup engine train
- ❑ 3 Teacup train cars
- ❑ 4 swings/chain sets for the carousel
- ❑ 8 bows for the carousel
- ❑ 3 fence pieces

# Royal Pony Palace

The largest of all Petite playsets, this set included a carriage, throne, banquet table, working elevator, battery operated light (activated by pushing down on a tower) and other items fit for Petite royalty. Two Petite Ponies were also included in this set. The colors of the accessories also vary in this set. **Collector's Note**: The snap-in bunting decorations on the turrets and elsewhere are removable and also very fragile from having been bent into position so they are very frequently broken.

- **Royal Pony Palace**
- **Sundrop** (crown symbol)
- **Magic Star** (wand symbol)
- 4 turrets
- Bunting strips (snap in plastic draped ribbons, in assorted sizes)
- Flag poles with flags
- 4 flags
- Grass/moat base
- Heart topper
- Swan car rider
- Dining table
- Dresser
- Poster bed
- Yellow single star pick
- Throne

$35 to $40

$5 to $10

$5 to $10

# Dream Beauties

Labeled as "all grown up My Little Ponies," Dream Beauties resembled horses more than ponies. Only six sets of Dream Beauties were produced (18 in total) in three different poses. They had long, brushable manes and tails, much like traditional My Little Ponies. Their bodies, however, were hard plastic. A row of pearly plastic beads ran down both sides of their manes. Dream Beauties were only available in Year 8. Like the Petite Ponies, Dream Beauties were all pegagus or earth ponies with no unicorns.

# Highflying Beauties

Highflying Beauties had large beautiful pegasus wings. Each wing was dual colored with the end portion of the wing painted in a pearly sheen. This group of Dream Beauties is the most desirable set amongst collectors.

$30 to $35

❑ **Wind Walker**
 ❑ Pink flower brush
 ❑ Lilies barrette

$30 to $35

❑ **Glider**
 ❑ Blue flower brush
 ❑ Purple lilies barrette

$30 to $35

❑ **Skyflier**
 ❑ Yellow flower brush
 ❑ Pink lilies barrette

# Rainbow Beauties

This set of Dream Beauties had multicolored hair and swirling rainbow inspired designs on the sides of their bodies.

$20 to $25

❏ **Morning Glory**
   ❏ Coral flower brush
   ❏ Purple hearts barrette

$20 to $25

❏ **Sky Splasher**
   ❏ Green flower brush
   ❏ Purple hearts barrette

$20 to $25

❏ **Windsweeper**
   ❏ Blue flower pick
   ❏ Yellow shooting star barrette

# Shimmering Beauties

Much like the Sparkle Ponies, this group of Dream Beauties had translucent bodies that were filled with glitter. The beads that line the Shimmering Beauties' manes were clear unlike other Dream Beauty sets that had colored beads.

$15 to $20

$15 to $20

- **Crystaline**
    - Purple flower pick
    - Dark pink lilies barrette

- **Dream Gleamer**
    - Mint green flower pick
    - Pink hearts barrette

$15 to $20

- **Stardazzle**
    - Yellow star pick
    - Mint green hearts barrette

# Showtime Beauties

Only two Dream Beauties made up the Showtime Beauty set. Each had a raised decorated saddle design, much like the Carousel Ponies.

- ❑ **Circle Dancer**
  - ❑ Purple wrapped candy comb
  - ❑ Pink "I Luv You" barrette

- ❑ **Mayfair**
  - ❑ Blue butterfly brush
  - ❑ Mint green "I Luv You" barrette

# Sweet Perfume Beauties

Each Sweet Perfume Beauty had a secret compartment under her metallic medallion symbol that held cream perfume.

- ❑ **Colorglow**
  - ❑ Pink flower pick
  - ❑ Periwinkle blue shooting star barrette

- ❑ **Colormist**
  - ❑ Blue flower brush
  - ❑ Pink hearts barrette

The My Little Pony G1 Collector's Inventory

- **Fair Flyer** — $20 to $25
  - Mint green flower brush
  - Purple hearts barrette

- **Song Rider** — $20 to $25
  - Purple flower pick
  - Mint green shooting star brush

## Trim 'n Grow Beauties

Trim 'n Grow Dream Beauties had hair that was meant to be cut. The forelock and the tail could be replaced with new hair that was included in the package. The majority of their mane was rooted into place and could not be replaced. Each Trim 'n Grow Dream Beauty came with a pair of scissors and 2 replacement hair pieces.

- **Mane Waves** — $25 to $30
  - Dark pink wrapped candy comb
  - Dark pink-purple bird and lily barrette
  - 2 locks of extra hair
  - Scissors

- **Sheertrimmer** — $25 to $30
  - Purple shooting star brush
  - Pink bird and lily barrette
  - 2 locks of extra hair
  - Scissors

Dream Beauties

$25 to $30

❑ **Spritzy**
  ❑ Periwinkle purple shooting star brush
  ❑ Purple bird and lily barrette
  ❑ 2 locks of extra hair
  ❑ Scissors

# Li'l Litters and Nursery Families

In the midst of Year 9, Hasbro released new and unusual friends labeled "from Ponyland." These friends were actually not ponies at all. Meet My Little Puppy, My Little Kitty and My Little Bunny.

# Li'l Litters

These adorable sets of Puppy, Kitty, and Bunny families came packaged on a bubble card with a brush or comb.

## My Little Puppy Li'l Litters

$5 to $10 each

- **Dalmatian Dots**
    - Dalmatian mother
    - White puppy with blue spots
    - White puppy with blue spots and blue ear
    - yellow puppies comb

$5 to $10 each

- **Lady Labrador**
    - Labrador mother
    - Purple puppy
    - Purple puppy with white chest
    - Coral puppies brush

$5 to $10 each

- **Pretty Poodle**
    - Poodle mother
    - Aqua puppy (head up)
    - Pink puppy (head down)
    - Blue-green puppies comb

$5 to $10 each

- **Sweet Spaniel**
    - Spaniel mother
    - Yellow puppy with white eye patch and freckles
    - Yellow puppy with white chest and muzzle
    - Blue puppies comb

# My Little Kitty Li'l Litters

Li'l Litters and Nursery Families

The names of Cutie Calico and Precious Persians seem to have been reversed on their packages based on their breed. Due to this fact, both are being named as their breed dictates, even though Hasbro reversed these names on the package. This is a factor to keep in mind if you are a mint on card collector.

$5 to $10 each

$5 to $10 each

- ❏ **Cutie Calico**
    - ❏ Calico mother
    - ❏ Blue kitten (waving)
    - ❏ Pink kitten (sleeping)
    - ❏ Yellow kittens brush

- ❏ **Dreamy Siamese**
    - ❏ Siamese mother
    - ❏ Pink kitten with purple accents (waving)
    - ❏ Pink kitten with purple accents (sleeping)
    - ❏ Magenta kittens brush

$5 to $10 each

$5 to $10 each

- ❏ **Happy Tabby**
    - ❏ Tabby mother
    - ❏ Purple kitten with white stripes (sitting)
    - ❏ White kitten with purple stripes (sleeping)
    - ❏ Blue-green kittens brush

- ❏ **Precious Persian**
    - ❏ Persian mother
    - ❏ White kitten (sitting)
    - ❏ Gold kitten with white chest (waving)
    - ❏ Peach kittens brush

# My Little Bunny Li'l Litters

$5 to $10 each

- ❏ **Adorable Angora**
    - ❏ Pink mother with bright pink tail
    - ❏ Light qua bunny with aqua eyes
    - ❏ Light purple bunny with purple eyes
    - ❏ Yellow butterfly brush

$5 to $10 each

- ❏ **Cuddly Cottontail**
    - ❏ Cream colored mother with purple tail
    - ❏ Yellow bunny with dark blue eyes
    - ❏ Pale blue bunny with blue eyes
    - ❏ Light pink butterfly brush

$5 to $10 each

- ❏ **Fancy Floppy**
    - ❏ Yellow mother with gold tail
    - ❏ Aqua bunny with purple eyes
    - ❏ Pink bunny with aqua eyes
    - ❏ Peach butterfly brush

$5 to $10 each

- ❏ **Happy Hopper**
    - ❏ Peach mother with blue tail
    - ❏ Dark aqua bunny with aqua eyes
    - ❏ Pink bunny with burgundy eyes
    - ❏ Purple butterfly brush

# Nursery Families

These cute sets of Puppy and Kitty families came packaged with themed accessories on a bubble card. These sets are much harder to find than the Li'l Litter sets. Several new accessories were introduced with the Nursery families sets that were later used in the Nesthackchen Baby Pony sets sold exclusively in Germany. Individual mommies and babies from these sets are valued at $10 and up each. Complete Nursey Family sets with all accessories are valued at $40 and up.

## My Little Puppy Nursery Families

- **Funtime Spaniels**
    - Spaniel mother (aqua and pink)
    - Aqua with pink accents puppy
    - Pink with aqua accents puppy
    - Pink playpen (smaller than regular MLP playpens)
    - Stack toy
    - Peach teddy bear
    - Blue lollipop brush

- **Scrub-A-Dub Spaniels**
    - Spaniel mother (pink with white paws)
    - Pink puppy (standing)
    - Lavender puppy (sitting)
    - White bathtub
    - Aqua scrub brush
    - White bar of soap
    - Blue moon comb

- **Sweet Dream Poodles** [not pictured]
    - Poodle mother (purple)
    - Purple puppy (standing)
    - Pink puppy (sitting)
    - Aqua cradle
    - Pink bottle (similar to Teeny Pony Twin bottles)
    - Yellow bottle (similar to Teeny Pony Twin bottles)
    - Lavender duck comb

# My Little Kitty Nursery Families

- **Slumber Time Siamese**
    - Blue mother with white accents
    - Blue kitten with white accents (sitting)
    - Blue kitten with white accents (waving)
    - Pink cradle
    - Pink bottle (similar to Teeny Pony Twin bottles)
    - Purple bottle (similar to Teeny Pony Twin bottles)
    - Purple crescent moon comb

- **Sudsy Angoras**
    - Pink and white mother with purple tail
    - White kitten with pink paws with pink heart (sitting)
    - Pink with white paws and white heart (waving)
    - Aqua bathtub
    - Yellow scrub brush
    - White bar of soap
    - Peach duck comb

- **Perky Persians** [not pictured]
    - Peach mother with aqua stripes
    - Peach kitten with aqua stripes (sleeping)
    - Aqua kitten with peach stripes (sitting)
    - Yellow playpen (smaller than regular MLP playpens)
    - Stack toy
    - Pinkish-purple teddy bear
    - Aqua lollipop brush

# Plush Ponies

Soft huggable plush versions of My Little Pony became available early in the My Little Pony timeline. While most of these cuddly plush ponies were manufactured by Hasbro under the Hasbro Softies label, a few were made by the Applause Company. Adult plush ponies stood about ten inches high and babies stand about seven inches high. All plush ponies had brushable manes and tails and plastic eyes. Many of the Hasbro Softies were available in two different poses. The plush ponies manufactured by Hasbro all had embroidered symbols, while the Applause plush ponies came in two different versions: one with embroidered symbols and one with printed symbols. **Collector's Note**: Do not put any pony plush into a clothes dryer and use heat as their hair will melt.

❏ Blossom

**Hasbro Softies Earth Ponies**

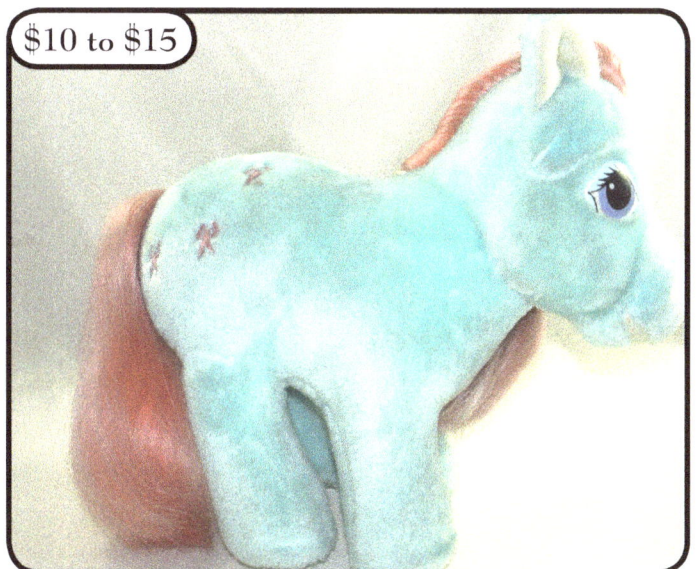

❏ Bow Tie

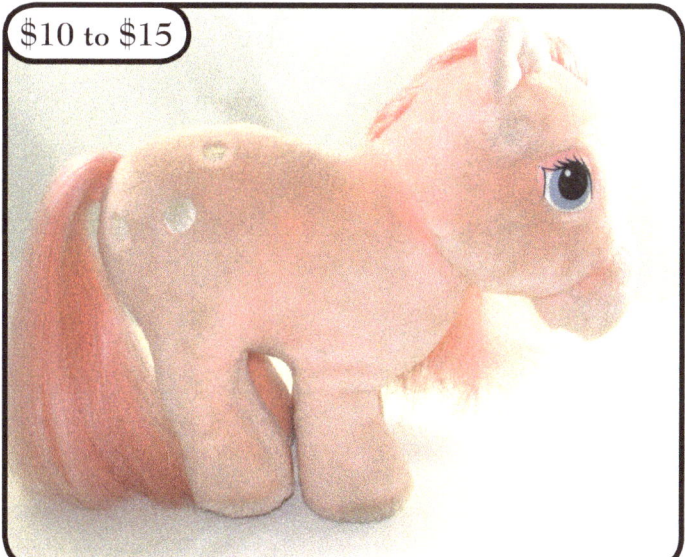

❏ Cotton Candy

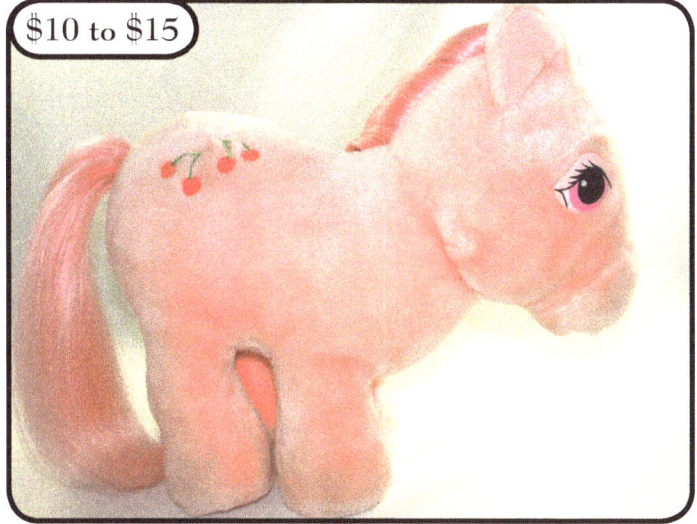

❏ Cherries Jubilee

❏ Posey

**Hasbro Softies Unicorn and Pegasus**
- ❏ Firefly (opened mouth)
- ❏ Firefly (closed mouth)

- ❏ Moondancer (closed mouth)
- ❏ Moondancer (open mouth)
- ❏ Glory

Plush Ponies

$10 to $15

$35 to $40

**Hasbro Softies Mother and Baby Sets**
- ❏ Lickety-Split (released alone as well as in set)
- ❏ Baby Lickety-Split

$15 to $20

$35 to $40

- ❏ Lofty
- ❏ Baby Lofty

$15 to $20

$35 to $40

- ❏ Surprise
- ❏ Baby Surprise

171

**Hasbro Softies Rainbow Ponies**
- ❏ Parasol (opened mouth)

❏ Parasol (closed mouth)

❏ Starshine (closed mouth)

❏ Starshine (opened mouth)

❏ Windy

Plush Ponies

**Applause Plush**
❑ Glory

❑ Firefly

❑ Cotton Candy

❑ Blossom

Printed Symbols — $20 to $25

Embroidered Symbols — $30 to $35

# Playsets

Alongside the pony releases, each year from 1983 on also featured playsets, buildings, furniture and appliances that served as residences or businesses and gave your ponies somewhere to go when bored in Dream Valley. Playsets often, but not always, included a pony and all came with many accessories. Many playsets were available for several years so they are listed here in the order that they first appeared.

Price Guide prices listed are for mint condition playsets that are complete with all accessories. Ponies and animal friends are also valued seperately.

The My Little Pony G1 Collector's Inventory

# Pretty Parlor

Released for the 1983-1984 toy line, the first pony playset was a Parlor where ponies could visit to get a new look. With a large mirror on the back wall and lots of racks for hanging accessories, the Pretty Parlor was the first of many MLP beauty shops. The Pretty Parlor building shape was reused several times in the history of MLP. Internationally, it was a kitchen while in the US it was released again as the Brush Me Beautiful Boutique. Hasbro also reused the building again in sets for the Littlest Pet Shop line and others. Twinkles is valued at $1 to $5 alone.

$15 to $20

$1 to $5

- **Pony**: Peachy
- Twinkles (orange cat)
- Pink heart brush
- Pink standard comb
- Rounded white yellow hat (**Variation:** white)
- Yellow flowered bonnet (**Variation:** white)
- Purple bridle
- Purple reins
- Purple saddle
- Pink cat carrier basket
- Purple strap for cat basket
- Pink blanket
- Yellow hair ribbon
- Green hair ribbon
- Name tags:
    - Peachy
    - Lemon Drop
    - Blue Belle
    - Butterscotch
    - Cotton Candy
    - Blossom
    - Minty
    - Snuzzle
- White hat rack
- White tack hooks

176

# Show Stable

The Show Stable focused more on the ponies as real horses. While later playsets gave them more human activities, the Show Stable had everything a pony needed for a horse show with several types of jumps and training equipment. In a fun touch, the flags on the Show Stable's roof were adorned with some of the symbols of the original set of Little Ponies. Originally released in 1983, this set was available in stores as well as through multiple mail order offers. The Megan's Place and Home Sweet Home playsets were essentially the Show Stable, but with different colors. Brandy is valued at $1 to $5 alone.

- **Pony**: Lemon Drop
- Brandy (brown dog)
- Yellow pony weather vane
- 4 flags:
    - Butterflies (yellow)
    - Heart (pink)
    - Flowers (green)
    - White stars (blue)
- Pink saddle
- Pink bridle and reins
- White bed (purple headboard)
- 3 white prize ribbons (1st, 2nd, & 3rd place)
- Pink felt blanket
- 2 green troughs
- 2 green window shelves
- 3 yellow trophy cups
- 2 white jump standards with yellow crossrail
- White A-style jump
- 6 green fence pieces
- Yellow heart-shaped grooming brush
- Purple standard comb
- Purple hair ribbon

# Waterfall

The Waterfall playset was a large white cloud with a friendly sun and rainbow background. It was designed to be a bathing place for your MLP. A smaller cloud over the pool served as a shower. When you pressed the button on the right side, water would sprinkle down from the cloud, while the left hand button created bubbles for the bath. It was available starting in 1983. Duck Soup is valued at $5 to $10 alone.

$5 to $10

- **Pony:** Sprinkles
- Duck Soup (orange duck)
- Pony Bubbles bottle and bubble solution
- Pink sun bath foam brush
- Pink handle comb
- 2 purple curlers
- Light green hair ribbon
- Blue terrycloth towel

$35 to $40

# Dream Castle

Dream Castle, released in 1983 and featured in all MLP movies and specials, was the original home of the ponies until it was destroyed by the Smooze in *My Little Pony: The Movie* and the ponies moved into Paradise Estate. The castle folded out to twice its size and featured several decorations and accessories. Features included a string and crank that allowed you to lower Spike in the basket and a similar system for lowering the drawbridge.

$40 to $45

- **Pony**: Majesty
- Spike the Dragon
- Yellow basket
- Blue trunk
- Blue damsel hat with colored ribbons
- Blue oval standing mirror
- Yellow crown
- 2 blue goblets
- Yellow table
- Purple cape
- Blue horseshoe stand
- 4 golden (yellow) pony horseshoes
- 2 yellow jumping hoops
- Blue throne (2 pieces)
- Pink blanket for throne
- 3 white flags with purple stickers
- 5 purple felt banners
- 2 yellow felt banners
- 2 hair ribbons
- Yellow shooting star brush (**Variation**: blue shooting star brush)

$1 to $5

$5 to $10

# Baby Buggy

The original Baby Buggy was released in 1984 and featured prominently in an episode of the cartoon series in which the furniture came to life and ousted the ponies from their home (*The Revolt of Paradise Estate*). It was available in stores as well as through mail order. In both releases the buggy came with Baby Cuddles, though Baby Cuddles herself changed between releases gaining Beddy Bye Eyes with the second issue. The carriage was large enough for the baby pony to stand or lay comfortably in and had a bar for the adult pony to push the carriage. The bar could lock into one of two height positions to accomodate all body types.

$5 to $10

$1 to $5

- **Pony**: Baby Cuddles

- **Pony**: Baby Cuddles (**Variation**: Beddy Bye Eyes)
- White buggy with pink umbrella
- Lace for buggy and umbrella
- Lavender teddy bear brush
- Bottle with lavender trim
- Purple rattle with white top and elastic
- Pink flowered pillow
- Pink flowered blanket
- Hair ribbon
- White diaper
- Pink bonnet with white polka dots
- Puffy sticker

$20 to $25

## Megan's Place

With lavender walls and a white roof and in the same mold as the Show Stable, Megan's Place was meant especially for Megan and her special friend, Sundance. This set was available exclusively at Sears stores between 1985 to 1986. This set is one of the most difficult sets to find complete. Snowball is valued at $15 to $20 alone.

$100 & up

❏ Snowball (white dog with pink accents)
❏ Turquoise weathervane
❏ 3 pink flags with white hearts
❏ Pink bed with white headboard
❏ Sundance's pink velvet bridle and reins
❏ 3 pink prize ribbons (1st, 2nd, & 3rd place)
❏ 2 white troughs
❏ 2 white window shelves
❏ 3 turquoise trophy cups
❏ 2 pink jump standards with turquoise crossrail
❏ Pink A-style jump
❏ 6 white fence piece
❏ Turquoise heart-shaped grooming brush

# Lullabye Nursery

First seen in *Escape from Catrina*, the Lullabye Nursery was the home of the baby ponies and the décor and accessories reflected that. The pony that came with the nursery, Baby Tiddly-Winks, was released twice, once with and once without Beddy Bye Eyes. The colors of some accessories changed from the original release to the version packaged with Beddy Bye Eyes Tiddly-Winks. This playset was available starting in 1984.

$5 to $10

$1 to $5

- **Pony**: Baby Tiddly-Winks
- Blue bath towel with blue trim & pink heart
- Purple rocker
- Yellow rattle with white top
- Baby bottle with pink trim
- Baby bottle with yellow trim
- Baby powder
- Blue bowl
- Pink BABY necklace with white text
- Light purple teddy bear brush
- Pink dresser
- 2 wooden blocks
- Blue mirror
- White cradle
- Blue mobile with pink animals
- Pink plush teddy bear
- Blue bathtub
- Pink swing
- Pink canopy for outside of the building
- Diaper box with 2 diapers
- Pink shelf with spaces for bowl and bottles
- Blue and white checked bow
- Tiddly-Winks puffy sticker

**Second Release**
- **Pony**: Baby Tiddly-Winks (Beddy Bye Eyes)
- Blue dresser
- Pink bowl
- Pink mobile with blue animals
- Pink bathtub
- Pink mirror
- Blue shelf with spaces for bowl and bottles

(All other items were the same as the previous release listed previously)

Playsets

$40 to $45

## Pony Purse

The Pony Purse was a simple set from 1985. It was a cloth purse with a special pocket, just the right size for carrying a special baby pony. The Pony Purse was later re-released with a different pony.

- **Pony**: Baby Sleepie Pie
- Pink and white pocketed purse

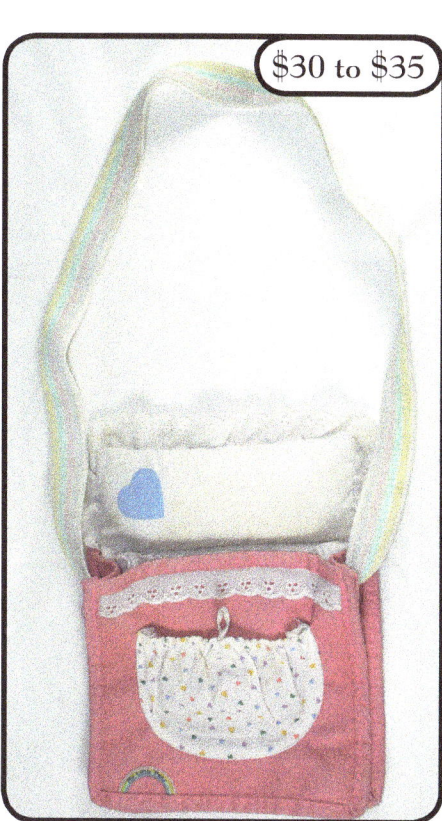

183

# Baby Bonnet School of Dance

Also featured in the TV series and movie, the Baby Bonnet School of Dance (shaped like a baby bonnet) was a ballet school with a full length mirror and a practice bar that came out as a part of the 1985 to 1986 line. The baby ponies could fit on three turntables on the fold-out stage. When you turned the wheel, the turntables would rotate, making the ponies seem to dance. The entire set folded neatly back into the bonnet and the bow on the top of the set became the handle for easy carry. It was also offered as a mail order in later years without Baby Half Note. **Collector's Note:** The connectors on the bow/handle are weak and are often cracked off or otherwise weakened from age so using the handle is not recommended.

$25 to $30

- **Pony:** Baby Half Note with Beddy Bye Eyes
- Yellow ballet dancer bee
- Pink ballet dancer bee
- Yellow ballet dancer swan
- Pink ballet dancer swan
- Yellow ballet dancer bunny
- Pink ballet dancer bunny
- Yellow ballet box (**Variation:** pink ballet box)
- Pink marquee
- Blue butterfly brush
- Pink flower tiara
- 4 pink legwarmers

- White mesh tutu
- Marquee posters
    - "Pretty Pony Prance"
    - "Swan Lake"
    - "Baby Bunny Bounce"
    - "Bumble Bee Boogie"
    - "Twinkle Toes Twirl"
    - "Woolly Wiggle Waltz"
- Scented body sticker

## Paradise Estate

One of the most lavish and largest playsets ever conceived, Paradise Estate was the ultimate pony home. This mansion, designed by the Moochick to replace the smoozed Dream Castle in *My Little Pony: The Movie*, had four rooms, a pool and more accessories than any other MLP playset. This set did not come with any ponies. Accessories are appropriate to their various rooms including a nursery, living room, kitchen and even an outdoor patio and swimming pool. Some accessories were sized specifically for Megan and not the ponies. This set was released as a part of the 1985 to 1986 toy line.

# The My Little Pony G1 Collector's Inventory

- Yellow crib (w/pink mattress)
- Yellow changing table
- Pink toy box with lid
- Duck pull toy
- Stacking toy
- 2 pink combs
- Pink perfume bottle
- Lavender floor lamp (w/white shade)
- Dresser with oval mirror
- Pink bed with purple headboard
- 2 Yellow speakers
- Stereo
- Lavender table lamp (w/white shade)
- Blue television set
- Lavender coffee table
- Lavender chair for living room
- Yellow sofa
- 2 pink long-neck bottles
- 2 pink milk cartons
- 2 pink spoons
- 2 pink knives
- 2 pink forks
- 2 pink glasses
- 2 pink heart dishes
- 2 lavender heart chairs
- Pink breakfast bar
- Lavender toaster
- Yellow refrigerator
- Pink sink/counter top/stove unit
- 4 ceiling fans
- 2 blue sea pony statues
- 2 white patio chairs
- 2 pink & blue lantern light
- Patio table with umbrella and heart topper
- 6 bunches of roses for the garden
- 6 bunches of purple and yellow flowers for the garden
- 4 bunches of pink flowers for the garden
- 4 bunches of lavender flowers for the garden

# Pony Purse
**(second set)**

In 1986 the pony purse got a slight make-over and featured a new little pony. Baby Crumpet was available with both a purple and blue symbol. The blue symbol is harder to find. Some collectors argue that the blue symbol may be the result of fading. The purse is valued at $40 to $45 without the pony. Price listed at right is for the set.

- **Pony**: Baby Crumpet
- Purple and white pocketed purse

$65 & up

$25 to $30

# Satin Slipper Sweet Shoppe

The Satin Slipper Sweet Shoppe of 1986, shaped like a baby's shoe, was an ice cream shop with Scoops the pony dressed like an old-fashioned soda shop clerk. The perfect place to stop and get a treat in Ponyland! In the mail order version of this set, Scoop's apron and hat uniform is darker colors.

- **Pony**: Scoops
- Purple standard comb
- Purple-pink ribbon
- White/pink/purple striped apron
- White/pink/purple hat
- Two-sided yellow specials board
- 3 mint green ice-cream sundaes
- 3 mint green floats
- 2 yellow chairs
- Round yellow table
- Yellow counter
- 4 yellow and mint green light fixtures

$5 to $10

The My Little Pony G1 Collector's Inventory

$40 to $45

## Perm Shoppe

The Perm Shoppe, shaped like a vanity table, complete with mirror, opened to reveal a hair salon with all the necessities. In addition to tons of hair care accessories, this set also came with a special container of Fifi's Fashion Foam, which was special holding spray for styling your pony's hair. It was released in 1986.

$40 to $45

$5 to $10

- Pink tray
- Pink ribbon rack
- Pink bow-shaped barrette
- Yellow bow-shaped barrette
- Purple flower-shaped barrette
- Mint green flower-shaped barrette
- Mint green towel bar
- 2 pink cloth towels
- Mint green salon chair
- Removable mint green sink
- Pink counter for sink
- Lace of outside of building
- Large pink plastic floor tray
- 3 pink ceiling lights
- Pink ceiling fan
- Mint green hanging sign
- 10 pink plastic bows for the outside of the building
- Pink standing heart shaped mirror

- **Pony**: Fifi
- Fifi's Fashion Foam
- Pink flower brush
- Mint green standard comb
- 3 eye shadow applicators
- Mint green eye shadow compact (with three colors: blue, pink, green)
- Pink mesh cap
- 3 large purple curlers
- 3 small purple curlers
- 2 thin purple hair ribbons tied to wide orange ribbons
- Pink smock
- Mint green counter with shelves
- Pink cash register
- Pink wall shelf
- Pink shelf for curlers
- Mint green beauty supply cart

# Poof 'n Puff Perfume Palace

Giving the Perm Shoppe and the Pretty Parlor even more competition was the Poof 'n Puff Perfume Palace, released in 1986. Shaped like a pink perfume bottle, the top of the building was meant to give your pony a spritz of perfume (scented air in this case) when squeezed. Though the building itself was relatively simple, it came furnished with tons of hair accessories.

### $30 to $35

- Periwinkle dresser
- Bottle of red nail polish
- Pink lipstick
- Pink mesh ribbon
- Yellow mesh ribbon
- Blue mesh ribbon
- Blue scarf with silver dots
- Pink plastic purse
- Magenta boa
- Turquoise hat
- Yellow "I LUV YOU" barrette
- Orange teddy bear barrette
- Bright pink flower barrette
- Blue starfish barrette
- Orange beaded necklace
- Dark pink beaded necklace
- Light blue toothed hairclip
- Blue butterfly brush
- Yellow standard comb
- Flower stickers (to decorate ponies)
- Pink cat hair pick with aqua hair
- Pale blue flower hair pick with light pink hair

# Brush Me Beautiful Boutique

The Pretty Parlor reopened under new management in 1987 as the building was repainted purple and renamed the Brush Me Beautiful Boutique. Though it came with many of the same accessories as the Pretty Parlor (including a cat, though in different colors), this set did not come with a pony (though one is pictured on the box). Catnip is valued at $5 to $10 alone.

- Catnip (white with aqua stripes cat)
- Pink grooming brush
- Pink standard comb
- Ribbons
- "Brush Me Beautiful Boutique" stand label
- Yellow round hat
- White hat with pink flowers
- Pink blanket
- Pink cat basket
- White strap for cat basket
- White saddle
- White bridle

$20 to $25

# Rock-a-Bye Bed

Introduced in 1989, the Rock-a-Bye Bed rocked from side to side like a cradle, but was made for adult ponies. With a special headboard that rotated to represent day or night, the set came with lots of nighttime accessories perfect for tucking your pony in for sleep.

- 2 large aqua hair curlers (**Variation**: lavender)
- Lime green crescent moon comb (**Variations**: blue, lavender, rose pink)
- 4 pink fuzzy slippers
- Soft printed blanket
- Pale pink pillow with white lace trim
- Pink diary
- Pink alarm clock
- Turquoise & white sleep mask
- Mint green & pink striped nightcap
- Spinning headboard wheel attached with a small pink piece

$20 to $25

# Scrub-a-Dub Tub

$20 to $25

While early ponies were content to use the Waterfall playset as an outdoor shower, the ponies replaced the raining cloud with indoor plumbing in 1988. The Scrub-a-Dub Tub was a small aqua bathtub with a shower curtain that a pony could use to either shower or take a bath in. This set came with everything a pony needed to get clean, including a rubber duckie. A year later, the tub was released in a pony gift pack called Scrub-a-Dub Gift Pack. In addition to the tub and accessories, the gift pack included a Sparkle Pony (usually Sky Rocket), a Merry-Go-Round Pony (Sunnybunch or Flower Bouquet), and a Sweetheart Sister (usually Spring Song).

- Bathtub with Sea Pony shower curtain
- White bar of soap
- Yellow shower cap
- White rubber duckie
- Blue star-shaped sponge
- Pink soap dish
- Pink towel

# Sweet Dreams Crib

$20 to $25

Just perfect for the littlest member of your pony family, the Sweet Dreams Crib was a simple white crib with a mobile and blanket to help tuck your baby pony in at night. **Collector's Note:** The mobile stand color may vary from the aqua one shown. Pink, yellow, and purple versions were also available. All versions seem to be equally common.

- White crib with yellow bottom and 4 aqua wheels
- Spinning pink & blue mobile with four hanging pony shapes (pink, purple, aqua, yellow)
- Printed blanket (yellow w/white & green stars, moons, circles, and pony)
- Aqua pillow with lace trim
- White bottle
- Pinkish-purple duck comb
- Lavender BABY necklace with yellow text
- Duck pull toy with aqua wheels and pink axles
- Pink rattle with aqua top

# Home Sweet Home

Home Sweet Home was yet another incarnation of the Show Stable. Released in 1989, this set came packaged in the original show stable box, but is called Home Sweet Home by collectors due to the sticker above the doorway which identifies it as such.

- Brandy (yellow dog with purple-pink accents)
- Purple-pink pony weathervane
- 4 yellow flags:
    - Stars (yellow)
    - Hearts (purple)
    - Leaves (green)
    - Kites (blue)
- Yellow bed with yellow headboard
- Light blue saddle
- Light blue reins
- 3 yellow prize ribbons (1st, 2nd, & 3rd place)
- 2 purple-pink troughs
- 2 purple-pink window shelves
- 3 purple-pink trophy cups
- 2 yellow jump standards with purple-pink crossrail
- Yellow A-style jump
- 6 purple-pink fence piece
- Purple-pink heart-shaped grooming brush
- Purple-pink standard comb

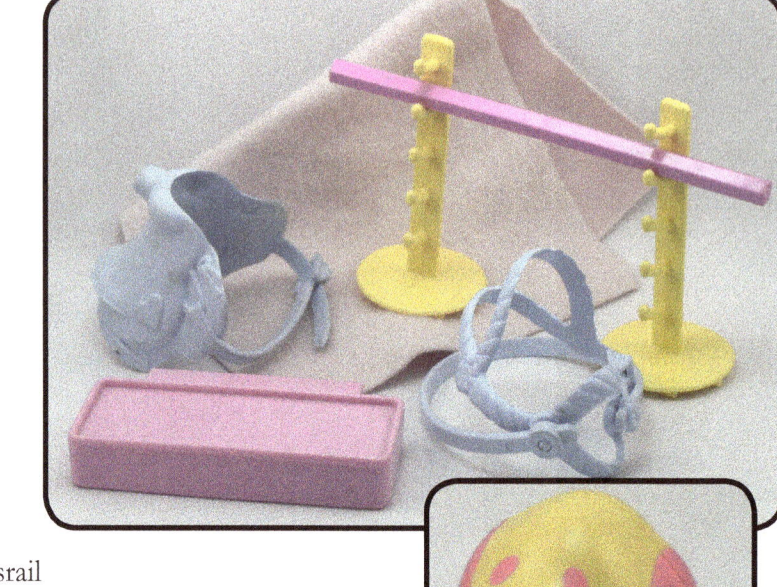

$15 to $20

$75 & up

# Dream Castle
**(second edition)**

A re-release of Dream Castle was available in 1989. It featured the same accessories as the original, but in different colors (including the building itself which was lavender instead of pink) and did not come with Majesty. Spike was included, but in a different shade of purple.

- Spike the Dragon (brighter purple and green)
- Pink basket
- Yellow trunk
- Yellow damsel hat with colored ribbons
- Yellow oval standing mirror
- Pink crown
- 2 purple goblets
- Pink table
- Blue cape
- Yellow horseshoe stand
- 4 pink pony horseshoes
- 2 pink jumping hoops
- Mint green throne (2 pieces)
- Light pink blanket for throne
- 3 pink flags with stickers
- Large pink felt banner
- Yellow flower pick
- Purple ribbon
- Magenta ribbon

$65 & up

$5 to $10

# Princess Baby Buggy

A new sparkly pink version of the Baby Buggy returned in 1988 with a new royal owner, Baby Princess Sparkle. She had a very detailed glittery castle symbol as well as a glittery star on her forehead. Baby Princess Sparkle was available with two different symbol colors: magenta pink and purple. The purple seems to be slightly harder to find than the magenta symbol version. Buggy with accessories but not pony is still valued at $55 or greater.

- **Pony**: Baby Princess Sparkle
- Dark pink carriage with sparkly pink umbrella
- Purple shooting star barrette (**Variation**: lavender shooting star barrette)
- White/silver floral lace ribbon
- Pink heart topper for umbrella
- Long pink ribbon for top of the umbrella
- Pink felt blanket
- Turquoise feeding dish
- Pink spoon
- Teal/turquoise sippy cup
- Dark purple duck comb (**Variation**: pink duck comb)

$30 to $35

$80 & up

# Pony and Accessory Cases

Though more of a storage solution than playsets, Hasbro released several carry cases over the years designed to hold either ponies, accessories or both. All were made by Tara Toy Co. **Collector's Note:** The plastic handle and latch are easily broken on any of these cases.

$10 to $15

### 1983 Show Stable Carry Case

Styled after the Show Stable, this carry case held 6 ponies in white plastic stalls and latches closed with a plastic pink clasp on the top. When closed, a pink handle on the roof made your ponies portable. The outside featured several ponies from Years 1 and 2 and also had blank name plates that were the perfect size for the pony name stickers. **Collector's Note:** There is a carry case that looks similar to this case that has a red roof (see inset) that was also made by Tara Toy Co (1987). Instead of MLP, this case featured horses in hats and other clothing and is labeled Kuddlee Ponee Carry Case. This is not an authentically licensed MLP item, but is the exact same size and model as the Hasbro version and can be used to store six MLP.

### 1985 Baby Pony Collector's Cases

This case was the only case ever made that was specifically designed for baby ponies. The case could hold nine baby ponies and closed via buttons on its right side. There is also a white plastic handle on the top. Unlike previous cases, which stored the ponies in plastic stalls, this case stores the ponies by having you lay them on their side.

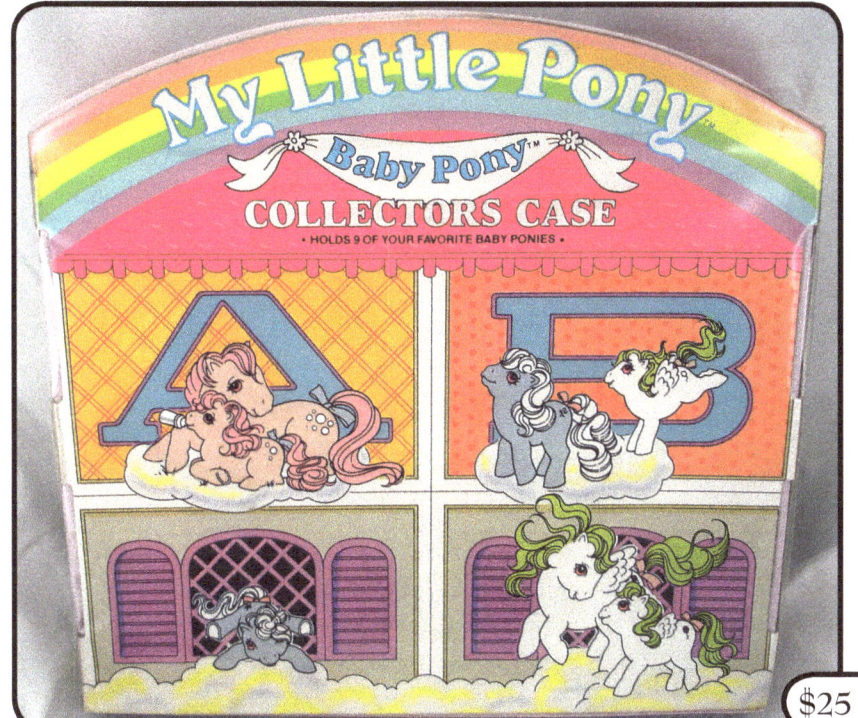

$25 to $30

The My Little Pony G1 Collector's Inventory

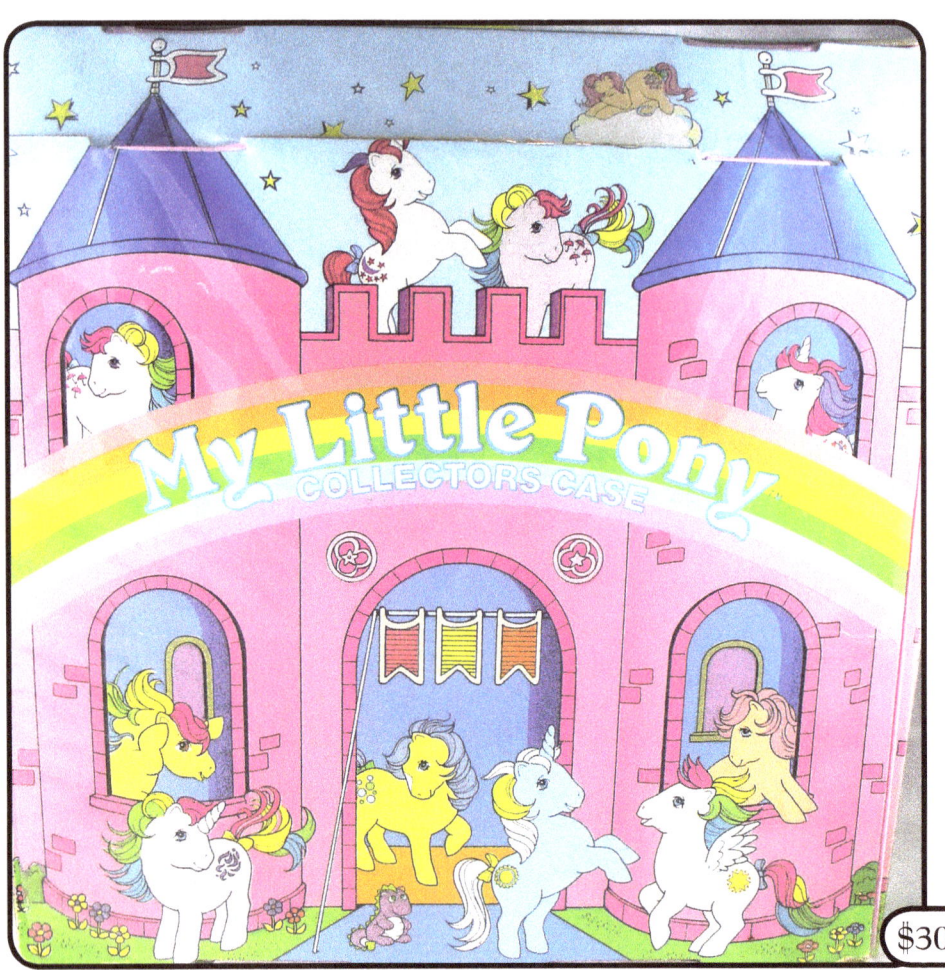

❏ **1985 Dream Castle Collector's Case**

Much larger than the 1983 case, this case was styled after the Dream Castle and could hold twelve ponies in white plastic stalls. In addition, this case also had a special cardboard drawer at the base labeled Pony Wear where a collector could store pony clothing and other accessories. It also had a yellow carry handle and plastic clasp, both of which were even more libel to break because of the weight of this case when full.

$30 to $35

❏ **1983 Accessory Cases**

Unlike the past cases, the cases in this set were not compartmentalized so the number of items they fit were up to you. Like a child sized set of luggage, they came in several sizes, all with a white plastic handle and latch. They could be used to store ponies, Pony Wear, brushes or other accessories. The complete set is valued at $40 & up.

$10 to $15 each

# Mail Order and Special Offer Ponies

While the majority of My Little Pony items were available in stores, some ponies were available only through special offers. In most instances, ponies could be ordered using special order brochures found in store purchased pony packages. Collectors could clip numbered horseshoe shaped Pony Points from pony packages and redeem them for exclusive offers. The number that appeared on a Pony Point corresponded with the value of that pony or set. Larger sets or playsets were worth a greater number of points than a single pony. Most of these offers also required money in addition to (or instead of) the Pony Points. In addition to mail order ponies, a few ponies were also available through certain brand exclusive offers with companies such as Kellogg, Current, and Chuck E. Cheese.

Due to the limited nature of these exclusive offers, mail order ponies are typically the most expensive and desirable of the My Little Pony collectibles. **Collector's Note:** The ponies in this section are much harder to find than store released ponies and, as such, their prices are more volatile when they do come up for sale. In the cases of very high value ponies, their value is indicated by the minimum price that they will sell for with the indication "& up." Ponies marked as such in mint condition can sell for far more than indicated at peak times.

Mail order and special offer ponies came with few accessories (if any) and arrived in plain cardboard boxes or sealed clear plastic bags. In addition to mail order exclusive ponies, some familiar ponies and playsets were re-released, sometimes unchanged, but often with variations from their store purchased counterparts. Most special offer ponies were offered in multiple brochures over several sequential years. For that reason, they are categorized within this book in the order that they first appeared. This section includes ponies that were available exclusively through special offer and does not include items that were released unchanged from their store versions.

# Ember, My Beautiful Baby Pony

The very first special offer pony, not to mention the very first baby pony ever offered, Baby Ember was available only through a 1983 mail offer. She was offered in three different colors. The purple version of Ember (with pink hair) was the version who stared in the film *Rescue from Midnight Castle* (later renamed *Firefly's Adventure* in re-release). A store bought version of Ember with purple hair and purple body and star symbol was sold as a part of the Listen 'n Fun series.

❏ **Blue Ember with blue hair**

❏ **Purple Ember with pink hair**

❏ **Pink Ember with purple hair**

# Birthflower Ponies

The Birthflower Ponies were a mail order offer that was available from 1984 until 1986. Each pony was in the pose of the original 6 ponies with pink hair and a white body. However, their symbols varied in shape and color depending on which month they represented. Each pony's symbol was the birthflower of your birthday month.

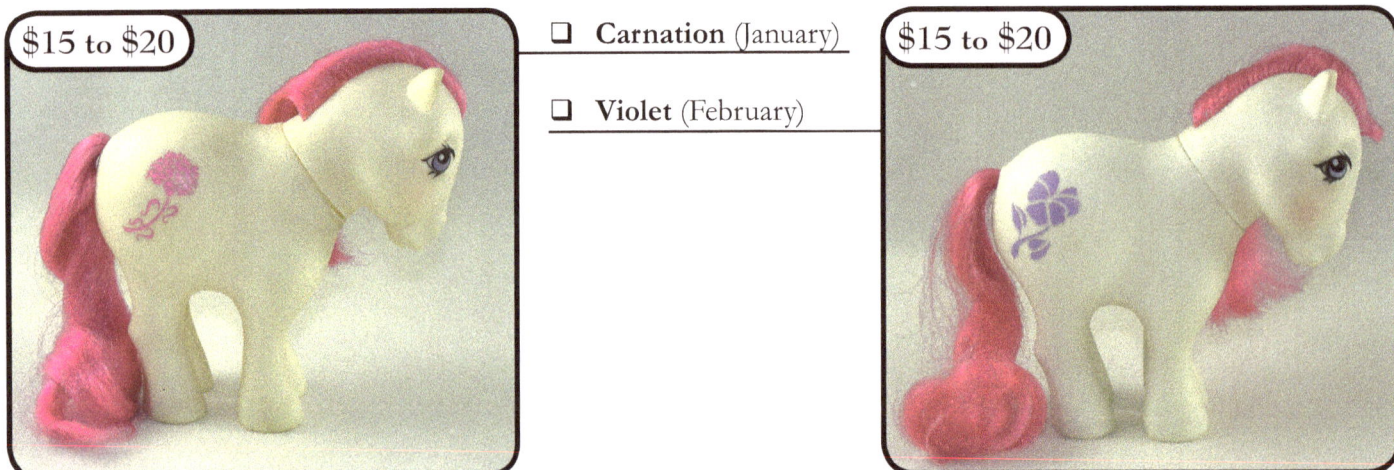

❏ **Carnation** (January)

❏ **Violet** (February)

# Mail Order and Special Offer Ponies

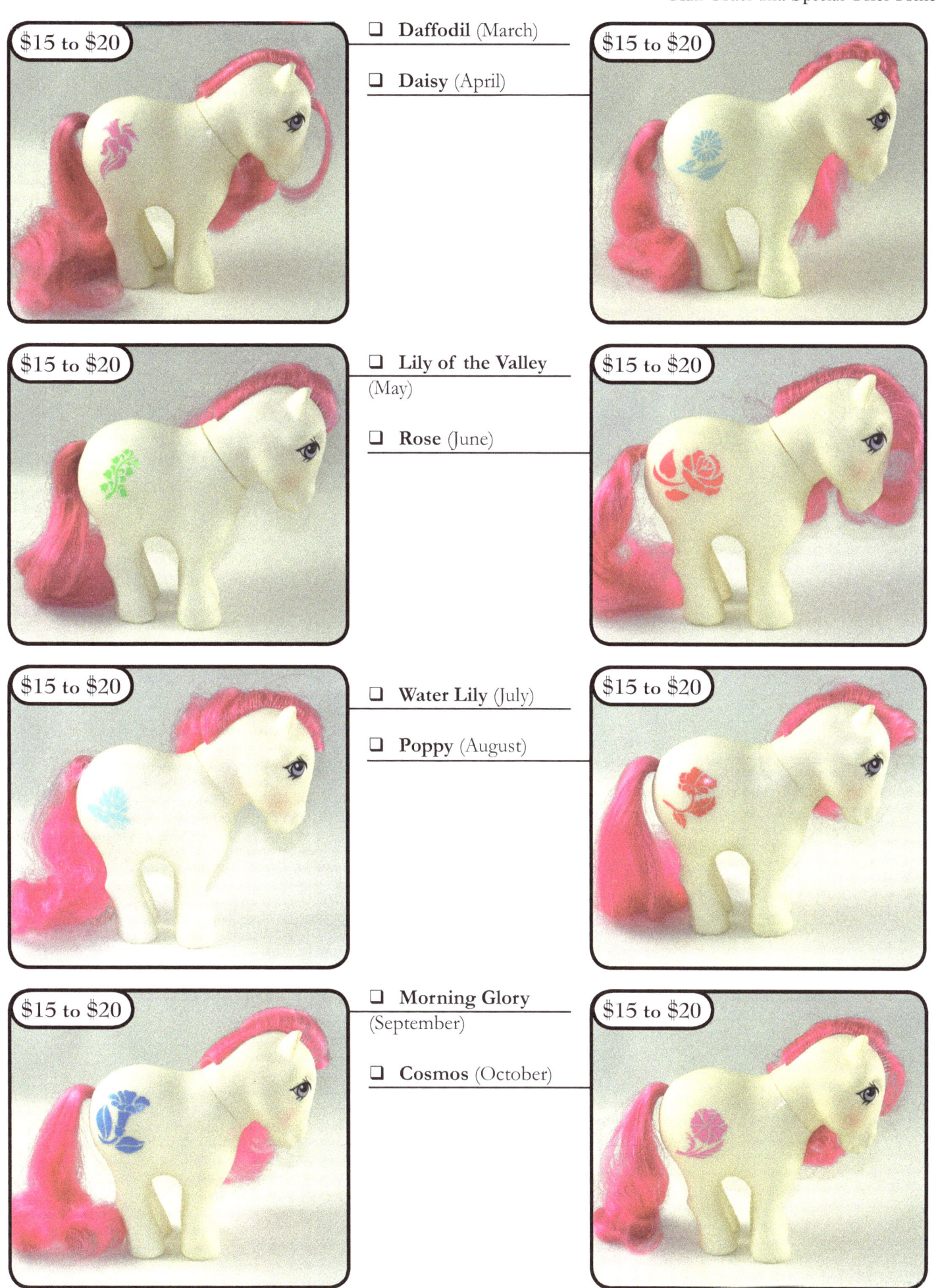

- **Daffodil** (March)
- **Daisy** (April)
- **Lily of the Valley** (May)
- **Rose** (June)
- **Water Lily** (July)
- **Poppy** (August)
- **Morning Glory** (September)
- **Cosmos** (October)

All: $15 to $20

The My Little Pony G1 Collector's Inventory

$15 to $20

$15 to $20

❏ **Chrysanthemum** (November)

❏ **Holly** (December)

## Li'l Tot Pony

Offered in conjunction with Toys for Tots, a person making a donation during this promotion would receive this pony as a thank you, while a needy child would receive one as well.

❏ Li'l Tot Pony

$25 to $30

## Collector Ponies

Early 1986 saw the original Little Ponies set return in a special mail offer. They were offered in multiple brochures until 1988. The brochures renamed these ponies the Collector Ponies. This set was different from the original in several key ways. For many ponies their colors were slightly different than the original release. The most noticeable difference, however, is the ponies' hooves. Instead of the flat feet of the original set, this set had concave hooves like all other pony sets. **Collector's Note:** These same six ponies were also released in 2007 in a special 25th anniversary set. The colors on the anniversary ponies are much brighter and richer than both the original and this release. Though the same mold as the ponies below, the 25th anniversary versions are considered part of the third generation of MLP because of their release date.

$1 to $5

❏ **Blossom**
  ❏ White standard comb
  ❏ White ribbon

❏ **Blue Belle**
  ❏ White standard comb
  ❏ White ribbon

$5 to $10

202

Mail Order and Special Offer Ponies

$5 to $10

- **Butterscotch**
- Pink standard comb
- Pink ribbon

- **Cotton Candy**
- Purple standard comb
- Purple ribbon

$1 to $5

$10 to $15

- **Minty**
- Blue standard comb
- Blue ribbon

- **Snuzzle**
- Blue standard comb
- Blue ribbon

$5 to $10

## Hollywood and Spike

To celebrate the release of *My Little Pony: The Movie*, Hasbro held a contest entitled "Who will save Ponyland?" where your entry was a guess as to which of the new characters from the movie (all introduced in the brochure) would save Ponyland. Along with this ad was a mail offer for Hollywood, the Flutter Pony (which should have been a hint, since the Flutter Ponies do save Ponyland) as well as a variation of Spike with larger eyes. The price listed below for Hollywood is for a pony in mint condition with wings. If her wings are broken or otherwise missing, she is still valued at $30 to $35.

$50 & up

$10 to $15

- **Hollywood**
- Dark maroon flower pick with pink centers
- 2 flutter wings with magenta tabs
- Silver metallic ribbon

- **Spike** (larger eyes)

203

The My Little Pony G1 Collector's Inventory

# Stockings, the Holiday Pony

In a special mailing to pony collectors towards the end of 1986 came an invite to a holiday party and, though most of the ponies in this offer had been previously available in stores, it introduced the first ever Holiday Pony. Stockings was only available through this offer.

❏ Stockings

$30 to $35

# Wedding Ponies

Throughout the years, various offers made mention of a pony wedding party, though different members of the wedding party were offered in different offers. Over the years there were three different versions of the bride (Satin 'n Lace), two identical but differently named grooms (Coat 'n Tails then Tux 'n Tails) and a ring bearer, Lucky (Satin 'n Lace's cousin, according to one offer).

$50 & up

$10 to $15

❏ **Coat 'n Tails (later renamed Tux 'n Tails)**
  ❏ White bow tie

❏ **Lucky, the Stallion**
  ❏ Purple bowtie
  ❏ White crescent moon comb

Mail Order and Special Offer Ponies

$15 to $20

❑ Satin 'n Lace (lavender version)

$60 & up

❑ Satin 'n Lace (magenta version)

$50 & up

❑ Satin 'n Lace (So-Soft version)

❑ White satin wedding gown
❑ White lace veil with silver
❑ 4 white bow shoes
❑ White lace garter
❑ Engagement ring
❑ Purple bird brush

# Blue Ribbon

Available in two different mail orders, each with different requirements, Baby Blue Ribbon was the master of ceremonies who came with the *Adventures in Ponyland* game. The game had no game pieces, as you were meant to use ponies to play. At the end of the game, Baby Blue Ribbon awarded her blue ribbon (that was included) to the winner. Adventure cards came in select MLP packages and collecting these cards made the game more interesting. Complete with all accessories, this set is valued at $85 & up. The poster is particularly sought after.

$30 to $35

❏ **Blue Ribbon**
  ❏ *Adventures in Ponyland* game board with poster on the back
  ❏ Pink paper dice
  ❏ Blue award ribbon

Mail Order and Special Offer Ponies

## Sparkle Ponies

Though the Sparkle Ponies were sold in stores, they were later re-released as a special mail offer with a few key differences. Though some ponies had a few cosmetic changes from their store bought sisters, like a change in hair color, the biggest difference between the sets is that each pony now had a second, smaller, version of her symbol on one cheek (in some cases on their non-display side). The mail order set of Sparkle Ponies is harder to find than the original and, as such, is usually worth more.

$15 to $20

❏ **Napper**
  ❏ Pink crescent moon comb
  ❏ Yellow ribbon with metallic trim

$10 to $15

❏ **Sky Rocket**
  ❏ Purple shooting star brush
  ❏ Pink ribbon with metallic trim

207

The My Little Pony G1 Collector's Inventory

$10 to $15

- [ ] **Star Dancer**
  - [ ] Yellow shooting stars comb
  - [ ] Blue ribbon with metallic trim

$15 to $20

- [ ] **Star Hopper**
  - [ ] Pink shooting star brush
  - [ ] Pale pink ribbon with gold trim

$10 to $15

- [ ] **Sunspot**
  - [ ] Bright orange sun pick
  - [ ] White ribbon with gold trim

$10 to $15

- [ ] **Twinkler**
  - [ ] Pink crescent moon comb
  - [ ] Pale yellow ribbon with gold trim

## Clipper

In the same Glitter Island mail offer that featured the re-issued Sparkle Ponies, was a freckled little boy pony named Clipper. He was the same body type as Lucky the Stallion rather than the Playtime Baby Brother Ponies style.

- [ ] **Clipper**

$30 to $35

# Pretty Mane Ponies

The Pretty Mane Ponies had long, horizontally-striped manes and tails and had smaller bodies like Flutter Ponies (though they did not have wings). They were offered separately (not as a pair) through a mail offer.

$60 & up

❑ **Dabble**
  ❑ Aqua shooting star brush

$60 & up

❑ **Scribbles**
  ❑ Pale yellow shooting star brush

# Baby Sisters

These sisters were offered through a mail order as a set and both are unicorns. Li'l Cupcake is a Newborn Baby while Li'l Sweetcake is a Peek-a-Boo baby pony.

$65 & up

❑ **Li'l Cupcake**

$65 & up

❑ **Li'l Sweetcake**
  ❑ Pink ribbon
  ❑ Dark blue ribbon
  ❑ White flower brush

/ The My Little Pony G1 Collector's Inventory

# Baby Pearlized Ponies

The Pearlized Ponies were a mail order re-release of the original set of Baby Ponies, but each one was covered in a shimmery glaze that made them pearly. They were each offered separately. For no apparent reason, Baby Moondancer is renamed Baby Moondreamer in this set, though every other pony's name remains the same.

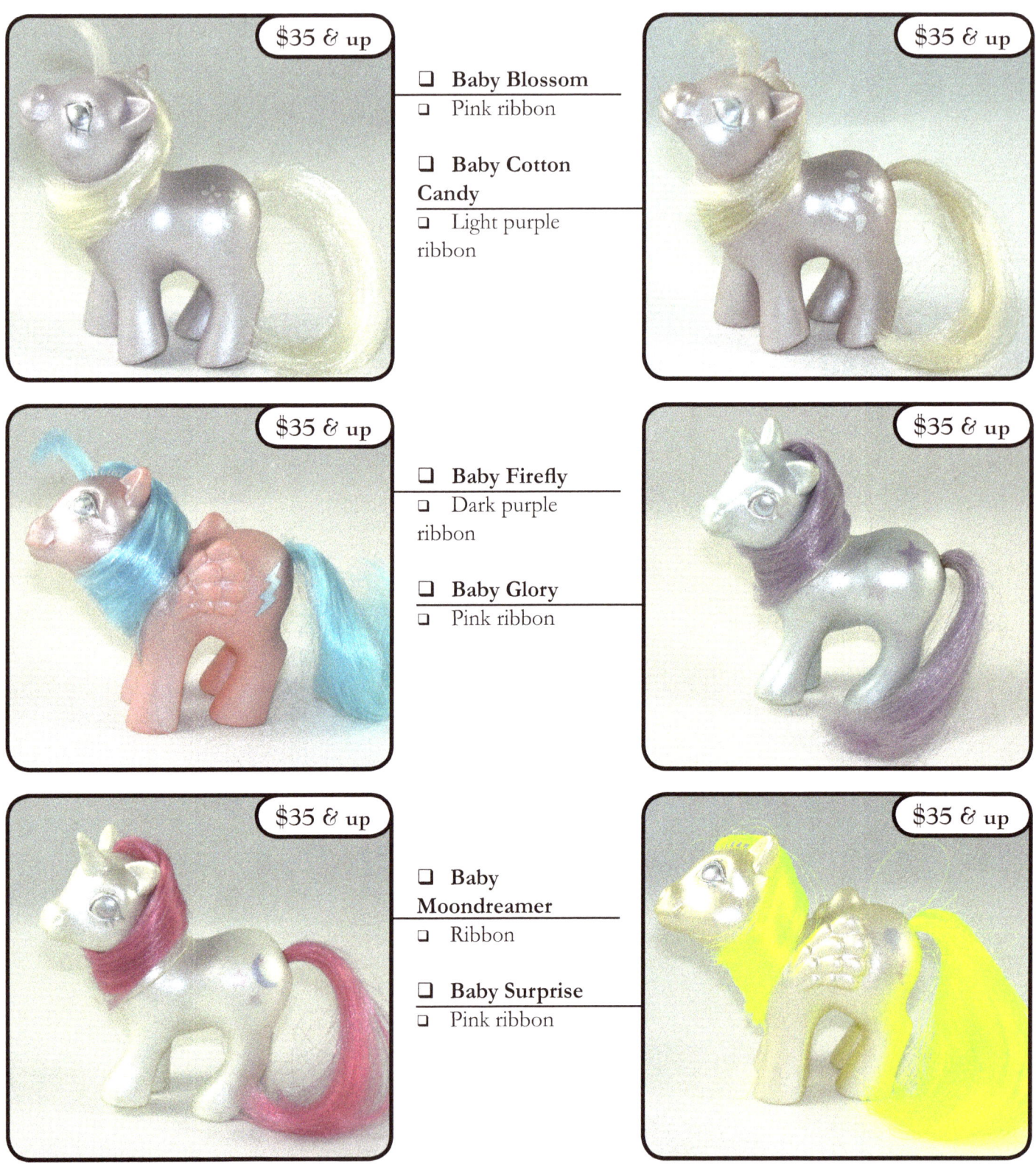

$35 & up

❏ **Baby Blossom**
❏ Pink ribbon

❏ **Baby Cotton Candy**
❏ Light purple ribbon

$35 & up

❏ **Baby Firefly**
❏ Dark purple ribbon

❏ **Baby Glory**
❏ Pink ribbon

$35 & up

❏ **Baby Moondreamer**
❏ Ribbon

❏ **Baby Surprise**
❏ Pink ribbon

210

Mail Order and Special Offer Ponies

# Playset Ponies

Since most subsequent mail offers had offered playsets but not their their original ponies, Hasbro re-released a set of ponies that had come only with playsets as a special mail order set. However, most were slightly different from the store version. Sprinkles came with a pink body instead of pale lavender and Baby Half Note and Tiddly-Winks were released with regular, not beddy bye, eyes. Tiddly-Winks also had no freckles. This Majesty's hairline started farther forward on her forehead than the original playset version.

$5 to $10

❏ Baby Half Note

$5 to $10

❏ Baby Tiddly-Winks

❏ Lemon Drop

$1 to $5

$5 to $10

❏ Majesty

❏ Sprinkles

$5 to $10

# Baby Birthday Ponies

Though in the "It's a Birthday Party!" brochure, the Baby Birthday Ponies were pictured as male ponies in the style of Lucky, they were actually female. They each came with several fun party accessories and were available separately through a mail order. Both had a Happy Birthday animal balloon symbol.

- Baby Sugarcake
    - Slice of pink cake
    - Yellow candle
    - Blue plate
    - Purple noisemaker
    - Pink ribbon

- Baby Gametime
    - Medium blue Pin-the-Tail-on-the-Pony game (Party Time is pictured)
    - Pink curly tail game piece
    - Pink straight tail game piece
    - Blue & white striped blindfold
    - Light blue ribbon

## Make-Up and Fashion Tote

In specially marked packages, throughout Year 7, pony fans could find a piece of Pony Make-Up. This make-up could not be purchased separately but was only available in pony packages. There were nine pieces of make-up altogether. **Collector's Note:** Pony Make-Up will stain your pony if left on too long. Always make sure to wash pony make-up off before putting ponies back in storage.

In addition, many packages of Year 7 also included a special mail away offer for the My Little Pony Fashion Tote, a bright pink bag designed to hold your pony make-up.

**Eye Shadow**
- Bubble Gum Pink
- Deep Sea Green
- Summer Sky Blue

**Lipstick**
- Petal Pink
- Seashore Coral
- Sunkissed Bronze

**Nail Polish**
- Crystal Coral
- Posey Rosy
- Tickled Pink

- My Little Pony Fashion Tote

Mail Order and Special Offer Ponies

# Twice As Fancy Baby Ponies

Though adult Twice As Fancy Ponies had been offered in stores, mail order was the only time that TAF Baby Ponies were offered. Babies of the original TAF set, these ponies were mostly identical to their mothers. In three cases, however, the baby is a different type of pony. Adult Milky Way was a unicorn while her baby is a pegasus. Babies Up, Up and Away and Sweet Tooth are also unicorns, even though their mothers were both earth ponies. Several TAF babies have a first tooth. **Collector's Note:** The ponies pictured below are marked Made in China. There is a variation of each pony below marked Made in Hong Kong. These variations have forelocks, while the China versions do not. Baby Milky Way's blue mane stripe is also in a different location (see inset).

- **Baby Dancing Butterflies**
  - Blue ribbon
- **Baby Love Melody**
  - Pale pink ribbon
- **Baby Milky Way**
  - Purple ribbon
- **Baby Sugarberry**
  - Pale yellow ribbon
- **Baby Sweet Tooth**
  - Light pink ribbon
- **Baby Up, Up, and Away**
  - Yellow ribbon

All: $60 & up

# Mommy Charms

Included in some My Little Pony packages were tiny plastic pony charms. Twenty different charms were available altogether. In addition, a special charm was available to members of the My Little Pony Fan Club and a matching charm was packaged with Sweet Scoops, the mail order pony, in the Pony and Pendant set.

- **Paint-A-Picture** blue with orange hair and a paint palette
- **Curtain Call** yellow with white hair and masks
- **Funny Face** purple with yellow hair and a clown face
- **Secret Keeper** white with yellow hair and a key
- **Sweetheart** pink with red hair and a heart and arrow
- **Sweet Tune** blue with purple hair and a tuba
- **Hugs and Kisses** pink with blue hair and x's and o's
- **Sweet and Special** white with pink hair and flowers
- **Pretty Please** purple with blue hair and a sugar bowl
- **Little Helper** dark pink with yellow hair and an apron
- **Tell-A-Tale** purple with pink hair and an open book
- **Fair Play** yellow with blue hair and a megaphone
- **Tiny Tumbler** orange with blue hair and a balance beam
- **Happy Dancer** blue with orange hair and tap shoes
- **Laugh-A-Lot** yellow with pink hair and question marks
- **True Blue** white with blue hair and a heart
- **Morning Sunshine** blue with orange hair and a sun
- **Yours Too** yellow with green hair and an ice cream soda
- **Fun Lover** white with purple hair and a party hat
- **Ticklish** pink with white hair and a feather

Mail Order and Special Offer Ponies

$15 to $20 each

## Fan Club Mommy Charm

- **Powder Puff** lavender with white hair and 3 purple hearts
- Charm hanger

$25 to $30

215

# McDonald's Bookmarks

A set of six My Little Pony bookmarks was available in McDonald's restaurants as part of a children's Happy Meal promotion. Each was a pony from the original My Little Pony set. These bookmarks resembled the Mommy charms, but also include an attached bookmark piece.

$25 to $30 each

- Cotton Candy
- Blossom
- Butterscotch
- Snuzzle
- Blue Belle
- Minty

# Pony and Pendant Pair

The mail offer only Pony and Pendant Pair featured Sweet Scoops and a matching Mommy Charm.

$180 & up

- **Sweet Scoops**
- White hair ribbon

$50 & up

- **Sweet Scoops Charm**
- Pink cord necklace

Mail Order and Special Offer Ponies

# Goldilocks

Available in a solo mail offer (most often packaged with Petite Ponies or Dream Beauties), Goldilocks had a body like a Sweetheart Sister Pony with hair in the ringlet curls of a Candy Cane Pony. She is named for the fairy tale.

- **Goldilocks**
  - Purple star brush
  - Bright blue ribbon

$15 to $20

# Rapunzel

Rapunzel, also named after the fairy tale character, had a long and curly mane and tail as well as tinsel in her hair. She is famous in pony collecting circles for being one of the most valuable ponies and has been known to sell for over twice the price listed below at peak times.

$400 & up

- **Rapunzel**
- Purple dots and hearts comb
- Pinkish-purple hair ribbon
- Turquoise "I LUV YOU" barrette
- Dark pink "I LUV YOU" barrette

217

# Valentine's Day Baby Ponies

Offered as an in-store offer from the stationary store, Current, which also sold MLP stationary and cards, these two unnamed ponies were offered as a Valentine's Day promotion.

$10 to $15

$10 to $15

❏ White w/red hair
❏ Pink ribbon

❏ Purple w/pink hair

# Mommy and Baby Pony Set

This mail order set featured a Mommy (with long curly hair) and a baby, both earth ponies, and several accessories. The baby pony is in the style of a Fancy Pants Baby Pony.

$150 & up each

Mail Order and Special Offer Ponies

- **Mommy**
- **Baby**
  - Bright yellow playpen
  - White squeeze bottle
  - Light aqua duck comb

## Chuck E. Cheese Baby Pony

$10 to $15

The Chuck E. Cheese pony could only be purchased or redeemed for tickets at Chuck E. Cheese restaurants. She was never available for purchase in retail stores or via mail order. Her symbol was a picture of the Chuck E. Cheese logo. She was packaged in a plastic bag with "My Little Pony" written across the front.

- **Chuck E. Cheese Baby Pony**

## Christmas Baby Pony

Christmas Baby Pony, the last mail order pony in this MLP generation, was not directly offered through a Hasbro mail offer, but instead was offered through specially marked boxes of *Kellogg's* cereal (most commonly *Rice Krispies*). With proof of purchase from specially marked boxes, you could send away for this unnamed holiday baby pony. (Because her symbol is a green stocking like that of Stockings, the Holiday Pony, this pony is often referred to as Baby Stockings, though that is not her official name.)

- **Christmas Baby Pony**

$1 to $5

# Pony Wear

A set of six outfits marked the beginning of My Little Ponies wearing clothes. These outfits were fairly simple compared to Pony Wear sets to come. All prices listed are for complete outfits in mint condition.

$10 to $15

- **Best of the West**
    - Pink saddle
    - White cowboy hat
    - Silver reins
    - Silver saddle blanket
    - Puffy sticker

$10 to $15

- **Great Skates**
    - 4 white skates
    - White headband
    - Pink and blue blanket
    - Pink saddle
    - Puffy sticker

$10 to $15

- **The Tea Party**
    - Straw hat with a pink ribbon and flower
    - 4 pink shoes
    - Floral printed cape

$10 to $15

- **Parade Pizzazz**
    - Feathered plume bridle and reins
    - Green, purple, and silver blanket
    - 4 pink shoes

Pony Wear

- **Pony Royal**
  - Magenta robe
  - Crown with ribbon tie
  - 4 lavender shoes
  - Puffy sticker

- **Sweet Dreams**
  - Terry cloth pink pajamas
  - Floral print night cap
  - 4 fuzzy slippers
  - 1 small curler
  - 2 large curlers
  - Puffy sticker

## Pony Wear
### (second set)

Sweet Dreams, Best of the West, Great Skates, and Pony Royal returned this year with four new outfits to create the second set of Pony Wear

- **Flashprance**
  - Rainbow striped mini dress
  - 4 pink leg-warmers
  - Purple MLP purse
  - 4 yellow bow shoes
  - Pink headband
  - Puffy sticker

- **Party Time**
  - Purple dotted dress
  - Party hat with printed circles
  - Present
  - 4 pink bow shoes
  - Puffy sticker

- **Pom Pom Pony**
    - White MLP shirt
    - Pink skirt with purple pleats
    - 2 pink and purple pom-poms
    - MLP pennant
    - 4 purple sneakers
    - Puffy sticker

- **Pony Luv**
    - White tennis dress
    - White tennis panties
    - Visor
    - Tennis racket
    - 4 white tennis shoes
    - Puffy sticker

# Pony Wear

### (third set)

This was the last set of regular Pony Wear outfits. In addition to four outfits from the previous Pony Wear sets (Flashprance, Party Time, Pom Pom Pony, and Pony Luv), four new outfits were available. Instead of puffy stickers, this set came packaged with flat scented body stickers.

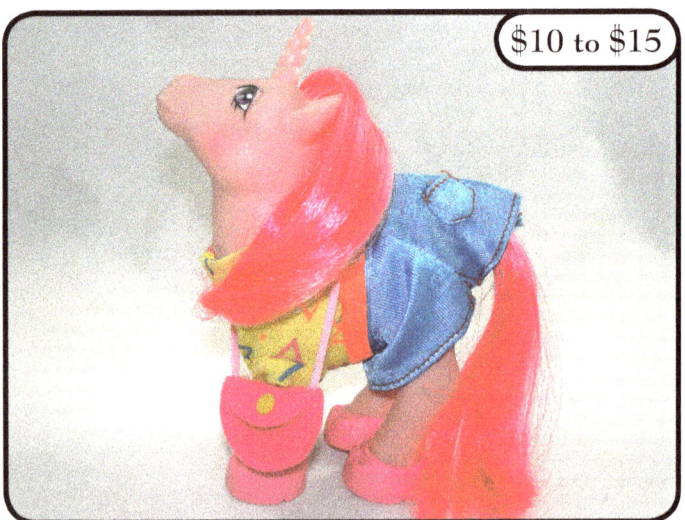

- **City Kids**
    - Yellow shirt with geometric designs
    - Blue skirt
    - Orange belt
    - Pink purse
    - 4 pink bow shoes
    - Scented body sticker

- **Neon Lights**
    - Orange and neon yellow dress with necktie
    - Black belt
    - 4 Yellow bow shoes
    - Scented body sticker

Pony Wear

- **Having a Luau**
  - Hawaiian shirt
  - Grass skirt
  - White hat with flower
  - Purple and orange purse
  - 4 white bow shoes
  - Scented body sticker

- **Strike Up the Band**
  - Yellow jacket
  - White skirt
  - Yellow hat with feather plume
  - Silver baton
  - 4 white sneakers
  - Scented body sticker

## Pony Wear with Jewelry

Many outfits in this set made an appearance in the *Escape from Catrina* cartoon television special. Each of these outfits included a special piece of jewelry for your pony to wear.

- **From the Designer Collection**
  - Magenta ruffled dress
  - 2 silver and pink drop jeweled earrings
  - Silver purse
  - 4 magenta bow shoe
  - Puffy sticker

- **Hearts and Candy**
  - Red and white lace dress with hearts
  - Red bonnet with lace
  - Jeweled red heart pendant necklace
  - 4 red bow shoes
  - Puffy sticker

- **Lights, Camera, Action**
    - Gold dress
    - White boa
    - Jeweled glasses
    - Gold choker
    - 4 blue bow shoes
    - Puffy sticker

- **Pageant Queen**
    - Silver evening gown
    - Jeweled tiara
    - "Miss Pony USA" sash
    - Silver purse
    - 4 lavender bow shoes
    - Puffy sticker

- **Something Old, Something New**
    - Wedding gown
    - Veil
    - Ring
    - Lace garter
    - 4 white bow shoes
    - Puffy sticker

- **Sweetness and Lace**
    - Purple nightgown
    - Purple sheer robe
    - Pearl necklace
    - 4 purple slippers with fur plumes
    - Puffy sticker

# Mother and Baby Wear

With the addition of Mother and Baby Wear sets, Mommy and Baby ponies could dress alike in matching outfits designed for all sorts of fun activities.

$15 to $20

- **Pony Workout**
- Blue hooded sweatshirts with stars on the collar (Adult)
- Blue hooded sweatshirts with stars on the collar (Baby)
- Blue sweatpants with stripes (Adult)
- Blue sweatpants with stripes (Baby)
- 4 gold sneakers (Adult)
- 4 gold sneakers (Baby)
- Puffy sticker

- **Prima Ballerina**
- Pink and white striped leotard (Adult)
- Pink and white striped leotard (Baby)
- Tutu (Adult)
- Tutu (Baby)
- 4 pink fuzzy legwarmers (Adult)
- 4 pink fuzzy legwarmers (Baby)
- 4 white bow shoes (Adult)
- 4 white bow shoes (Baby)
- Puffy sticker

$15 to $20

- **Sun and Fun**
- Yellow bikini swimsuit (Adult)
- Yellow bikini swimsuit (Baby)
- Pink sunhat (Adult)
- Pink sunhat (Baby)
- Striped blanket (Adult)
- Striped blanket (Baby)
- Puffy sticker

$15 to $20

- **Sunday Stroll**
- Pink floral print dress (Adult)
- Pink floral print dress (Baby)
- Lace bonnet (Adult)
- Lace bonnet (Baby)
- Purse (Adult)
- Purse (Baby)
- 4 pink bow shoes (Adult)
- 4 pink bow shoes (Baby)
- Puffy sticker

$15 to $20

Pony Wear

- **Ready for Rainbows**
- Yellow rain slicker (Adult)
- Yellow rain slicker (Baby)
- Yellow rain hat (Adult)
- Yellow rain hat (Baby)
- 2 purses
- 4 red rain boots (Adult)
- 4 red rain boots (Baby)
- Puffy sticker

$15 to $20

$15 to $20

- **Snow Angels**
- Pink skating outfit with fur trim (Adult)
- Pink skating outfit with fur trim (Baby)
- Winter hat (Adult)
- Winter hat (Baby)
- 4 white ice skates (Adult)
- 4 white ice skates (Baby)
- Puffy sticker

# Baby Pony Wear with Pocket Pals

After much anticipation, Baby Ponies finally had their own line of Pony Wear that included cute little pompom Pocket Pals that fit snuggly into the pockets of their outfits. Two outfits were packaged together in each pack with a flat scented body sticker showing ponies wearing the outfits.

227

$5 to $10

### Overalls and Bunny Suit
- **Bunny Suit**
  - White bunny costume
  - Bunny pal
  - Scented body sticker

- **Overalls**
  - Pink overalls with white shirt
  - Pink hat
  - 4 yellow bow shoes
  - Doll pal

$5 to $10

$5 to $10

### Jumper and Snowsuit
- **Jumper**
  - Red jumper with striped shirt
  - 4 yellow bow shoes
  - Kitty pal (white)

- **Snowsuit**
  - Striped snowsuit
  - Snowman pal
  - Scented body sticker

$5 to $10

$5 to $10

### Bathrobe and Clown Suit
- **Bathrobe**
  - Yellow and white bathrobe
  - Shower cap
  - Duck pal

- **Clown Suit**
  - Multicolored clown costume
  - Silver mask
  - 4 yellow bow shoes
  - Clown pal
  - Scented body sticker

$5 to $10

$5 to $10

### Dragon Suit and Sunsuit
- **Dragon Suit**
  - Dragon costume
  - Dragon pal

- **Sunsuit**
  - Floral and blue outfit
  - Blue bonnet
  - Frog pal
  - Scented body sticker

$5 to $10

# Pony Wear with Pocket Pals

### (second set)

In addition to the outfits available in the first set of Baby Pony Wear with Pocket Pals, two new packs (four new outfits) were offered to create a new set.

- **Lion Suit**
  - Lion costume
  - Kitty pal (orange)

- **Sleepwear**
  - Orange floral printed nightgown
  - Orange floral printed nightcap
  - 4 fuzzy green slippers
  - Teddy bear pal
  - Scented body sticker

**Elephant Suit and Party Dress**

- **Elephant Suit**
  - Elephant costume
  - Mouse pal

- **Party Dress**
  - White dress with floral print
  - 4 pink bow shoes
  - Puppy pal
  - Scented body sticker

$5 to $10 (each)

## Megan and Pony Wear

This set allowed Megan and Sundance (or any other pony) to wear matching outfits. The Country Jamboree outfit matched the outfit that the character of Megan wore in the cartoon series and is especially popular.

$15 to $20

- **Picnic in the Park**
  - Denim dress with attached red and white shirt
  - Denim pony cape with red and white heart trim
  - Red heart shoes (Megan)
  - 4 red bow shoes (pony)
  - Red ribbon
  - Scented body sticker

$25 to $30

- **Country Jamboree**
    - Green overalls
    - Pink and white striped shirt
    - Green pony cape with pink and white trim
    - Pink heart shoes (Megan)
    - 4 pink bow shoes (pony)
    - Pink ribbon
    - Scented body sticker

$15 to $20

- **Ice Princesses**
    - Pink coat with fur trim
    - Purple leggings
    - Pony coat with fur trim
    - Pink ice skates (Megan)
    - White ribbon
    - Scented body sticker

$15 to $20

- **Flower Darlings**
    - Blue dress with flowers and lace trim
    - Lace headpiece
    - Blue pony dress with flowers
    - White heart shoes (Megan)
    - 4 white bow shoes (pony)
    - Scented body sticker

$15 to $20

- **By the Sea**
    - Blue bathing suit
    - Magenta beach cape with ribbon trim
    - Blue pony beach cape
    - Purple sunglasses (Megan)
    - Purple ribbon
    - Scented body sticker

# Pony Wear

- **Sweet Dreams**
  - White floral print nightgown
  - White pony nightgown
  - Lavender heart shoes (Megan)
  - 4 lavender bow shoes (pony)
  - Lavender ribbon
  - Scented body sticker

$15 to $20

## Play 'N Wear

The Play 'N Wear set offered unique accessories in addition to fun outfits designed for all types of activities.

$15 to $20

- **Sidewalk Surfer**
  - Dress with gold waistband
  - Gold visor
  - Headphones
  - 2 gold knee pads
  - Skateboard

$15 to $20

- **Pretty As A Picture**
  - Artist shirt
  - Blue pants
  - Beret
  - 4 red bow shoes
  - Paint pallet
  - Paintbrush

- **Milk 'N Cookies**
  - Kitty printed nightgown
  - Kitty printed nightcap
  - Blanket
  - Pillow
  - Cup
  - Cookie plate

- **Pony Holiday**
  - Yellow floral print dress
  - Straw hat
  - 4 magenta bow shoes
  - Suitcase

- **Hit The Slopes**
  - Pink ski pants
  - Knitted hat
  - Ski goggles
  - Skis

- **Get Into The Groove**
  - Yellow and dark aqua dress
  - 4 dark aqua socks
  - Yellow hairclip
  - 4 yellow bow shoes
  - Radio

# Costume Wear

Thanks to this set, My Little Ponies could dress up in sparkling outfits for costume parties or glamorous events.

- **Abra-Ca-Dabra**
    - Gold top with sheer sleeves
    - Shiny pants
    - Sheer veil
    - Hair band
    - 4 gold slippers

- **Rockin' The Night Away**
    - Purple shirt with multicolored collar
    - Shiny pants
    - Headband
    - 2 multicolored gloves
    - 2 purple bow shoes
    - Guitar

- **Academy Award**
    - Silver gown with blue and magenta trim
    - Magenta and blue mesh headpiece
    - 4 silver glitter bow shoes

- **Pony-Naut**
    - Spacesuit
    - Silver and gold backpack
    - Plastic helmet
    - 4 silver glitter bow shoes

$15 to $20

- **Galaxy Glamour**
    - Gold metallic shirt
    - Silver pants
    - Headband
    - Rocket pack
    - 4 silver glitter bow shoes

$15 to $20

- **In The Center Ring**
    - Metallic bodysuit
    - Lace trimmed cape
    - Plumed headpiece
    - Mask
    - 4 purple bow shoes

## Pretty Ups

Much like the Pony Wear sets, the Pretty Ups sets were meant to help collectors make their ponies even more beautiful. Released in 1987, each set included a variety of themed barrettes, clips, a brush or comb, and a ribbon.

$15 to $20

### Birds and Flowers
- Green lilies barrette
- Dark pink lilies barrette
- Dark yellow bird and lily barrette
- Lavender bird and lily barrette
- Purple bow clip with pink hair
- White flower pick with dark pink hair
- Blue bird pick with yellow hair and tinsel
- White/mint ribbon
- Blue butterfly brush

Pony Wear

$15 to $20

### Kittens and Teddies
- Dark aqua teddies barrette
- Light pink teddies barrette
- Yellow puppy barrette
- Blue puppy barrette
- Blue bow clip with purple hair
- Purple kitten pick with pink hair
- Yellow puppy pick with aqua hair and multicolored tinsel
- Coral ribbon
- Pink duck comb

$15 to $20

### Ribbons and Lace
- Blue "I Luv You" barrette
- Pink "I Luv You" barette
- Mint green oval barrette
- Purple oval barrette
- Purple-pink bow clip with aqua hair
- Dark aqua bow pick with bright yellow hair
- Pink bow pick with white hair and gold tinsel
- Light blue/aqua ribbon
- Lavender bird brush

$15 to $20

### Seashore
- Green fish barrette
- Blue fish barrette
- Pink sand dollar barrette
- Yellow sand dollar barrette
- Aqua bow clip with pink hair
- Light blue shell pick with aqua hair
- Coral shell pick with chartreuse hair
- Bright yellow ribbon
- Green fish comb

# Stickers

In addition to the My Little Ponies themselves and their seemingly endless supply of accessories, stickers were also included in many early pony packages. These stickers took the form of either a round puffy sticker or a flat scented body sticker. Both types of stickers bore the image of a My Little Pony with that pony's name printed underneath. In most cases, the pony on the sticker matched the pony with which it was packaged.

**Collector's Note:** Stickers are worth significantly more if they are on their original backing and more still if they are in their original plastic sleeve. Puffy stickers have the tendency to have their layers pull apart and this greatly decreases their value. The Adult Sea Pony stickers command much higher prices than other US stickers.

## 1983-1984 Stickers

❏ Applejack    ❏ Blossom    ❏ Bow Tie (puple hair)    ❏ Bubbles

❏ Cotton Candy    ❏ Seashell    ❏ Firefly    ❏ Glory

❏ Medley    ❏ Moondancer    ❏ Sunbeam    ❏ Twilight

Stickers

| | | | |
|---|---|---|---|
| ☐ Moonstone | ☐ Parasol | ☐ Skydancer | ☐ Starshine |

☐ Sunlight   ☐ Windy

## 1984-1985 Stickers

☐ Bow Tie (pink hair)   ☐ Cherries Jubilee   ☐ Lickety-Split   ☐ Posey

☐ Tootsie   ☐ Gusty (pink bow)   ☐ Gusty (purple bow)   ☐ Gusty (pink hair stripe)

The My Little Pony G1 Collector's Inventory

☐ Heart Throb ☐ Powder (lighter) ☐ Powder (darker) ☐ Skyflier

☐ Sparkler (pink stripe) ☐ Sparkler (red stripe) ☐ Surprise (pink bow) ☐ Surprise (purple bow)

☐ Surprise (green hair) ☐ Starflower ☐ Pinwheel ☐ Trickles

☐ Confetti ☐ Tickle ☐ Flutterbye ☐ Baby Blossom

Stickers

☐ Baby Cotton Candy ☐ Baby Firefly ☐ Baby Glory ☐ Baby Moondancer

☐ Baby Surprise ☐ High Tide ☐ Sand Dollar ☐ Seabreeze

☐ Sea Mist ☐ Wave Jumper ☐ Whitecap ☐ Backstroke

☐ Sea Shimmer ☐ Sea Star ☐ Splasher ☐ Surf Rider

The My Little Pony G1 Collector's Inventory

- Tiny Bubbles
- Baby Cuddles (white lace)
- Baby Cuddles (blue lace)
- Megan and Sundance (pink bridle)

- Megan and Sundance (blue bridle)
- Baby Tiddley-Winks

## 1985-1986 Stickers

- Bouncy
- Buttons
- Cherries Jubilee
- Cupcake

- Fifi
- Gusty (blue hair)
- Gusty (green hair)
- Heart Throb

240

Stickers

❏ Hippity-Hop ❏ Lickety-Split ❏ Lofty ❏ Magic Star

❏ North Star ❏ Paradise ❏ Posey ❏ Scrumptious

❏ Shady ❏ Skippity-Doo ❏ Surprise ❏ Truly

❏ Twist ❏ Wind Whistler ❏ Fizzy ❏ Galaxy
❏ Ribbon (not pictured)

❏ Gingerbread ❏ Masquerade ❏ Sky Rocket ❏ Speedy

241

The My Little Pony G1 Collector's Inventory

☐ Sweet Pop  ☐ Sweet Stuff  ☐ Whizzer  ☐ Baby Gusty

☐ Baby Heart Throb  ☐ Baby Lickety-Split  ☐ Baby Lofty  ☐ Baby Ribbon

☐ Baby Shady  ☐ Forget-Me-Not  ☐ Honeysuckle  ☐ Lily

☐ Morning Glory  ☐ Peach Blossom  ☐ Rosedust  ☐ Beachcomber

☐ Ripple  ☐ Sea Shimmer  ☐ Sunshower  ☐ Surf Rider

Stickers

- [ ] Water Lily
- [ ] Best Wishes
- [ ] Baby Cuddles
- [ ] Baby Half Note

- [ ] Megan and So Soft Sundance
- [ ] Molly and Baby Sundance
- [ ] Baby Sleepy Pie
- [ ] Baby Tiddley-Winks

- [ ] Best of the West
- [ ] Great Skates
- [ ] Pony Royal
- [ ] Sweet Dreams

- [ ] Flashprance
- [ ] Party Time
- [ ] Pom Pom Pony
- [ ] Pony Luv

The My Little Pony G1 Collector's Inventory

- ☐ From the Designer Collection
- ☐ Hearts and Candy
- ☐ Lights, Camera, Action!
- ☐ Pageant Queen
- ☐ Something Old, Something New
- ☐ Sweetness and Lace
- ☐ Ready For Rainbows
- ☐ Snow Angels
- ☐ Sunday Stroll
- ☐ Sun and Fun
- ☐ Pony Workout
- ☐ Prima Ballerinas
- ☐ Flashprance
- ☐ Party Time
- ☐ Pom Pom Pony
- ☐ Pony Luv

244

Stickers

❏ City Kids ❏ Having a Luau ❏ Neon Lights ❏ Strike Up the Band

❏ Clown outfit and Bathrobe ❏ Dragon suit and Sunsuit ❏ Overalls and Bunny suit ❏ Snowsuit and Jumper

❏ By the Sea ❏ Country Jamboree ❏ Flower Darlings ❏ Ice Princess

❏ Picnic in the Park ❏ Sweet Dreams

# Other Licensed Merchandise

In addition to the My Little Pony toys we all know and love, Hasbro licensed hundreds of other My Little Pony products. Items such as clothing, books, games, lunchboxes, charms, stamps. puzzles, party supplies, books, bedding, electronics, beauty items, dishware, clocks, and stationary products all sported a My Little Pony logo or image. While these items are highly collectible, they are simply too numerous to cover in this book. My Little Pony licensed merchandise can vary greatly in price according to the item.

# Index

**Symbols**

4-Speed 54

**A**

Abra-Ca-Dabra 233
Academy Award 233
Adorable Angora 166
Angel 62
Apple Delight Family 94
Applejack 22, 28

**B**

Baby 219
Baby Bonnet School of Dance 184
Baby Buggy 180
Baby Ember 200
Backstroke 35
Banana Surprise 82
Bangles 62
Barnacle 70
Bathrobe and Clown Suit 228
Baby Beach Ball 134
Beachball 104
Beachcomber 46
Beautybloom 124
Best of the West 220
Best Wishes 47
Big Top 75
Birds and Flowers 234
Birthday Pony 130
Baby Blossom 32, 210
Blossom 20, 22, 169, 173, 202
Blue Belle 20, 202
Blueberry Baskets 83
Blue Ribbon 206
Bonnie Bonnets 84
Bootsie 138
Baby Bouncy 52
Bouncy 38
Bouquet 71
Bow-Tie 22, 28
Baby Bows 88
Bow Tie 169
Boysenberry Pie 83
Braided Beauty 71
Brandy 177, 194
Bridal Beauty 130
Bright Bouquet Family 95
Baby Brightbow 121
Bright Eyes 66
Brightglow 122
Bright Night 112
Brilliant Bloom 101
Brilliant Blossoms 96
Brush Me Beautiful Boutique 191
Bubblefish 123
Bubbles 22
Bunkie 76
Bunny Hop 123
Butterscotch 20, 203
Buttons 38, 84
Buzzer 80
By the Sea 230

**C**

Caramel Crunch 91
Carnation 200
Celebrate 47
Cha Cha 114
Cha Cha the Llama 78
Chatterbox 139
Cherries Jubilee 28, 38, 169
Cherry Treats 83
Chief 70
Chocolate Delight 135
Christmas Baby Pony 219
Chrysanthemum 202
Chuck E. Cheese Baby Pony 219
Circle Dancer 159
City Kids 222
Clipper 208
Cloud Dreamer 74
Cloud Puff 55
Coat 'n Tails 204
Coco Berry 82
Colorglow 159
Colormist 159
Confetti 31
Cool Breeze 107
Cosmos 201
Baby Cotton Candy 32, 210
Cotton Candy 20, 22, 169, 173, 203
Baby Countdown 99
Country Jamboree 230
Cranberry Muffins 83
Creamsicle the Giraffe 56
Baby Crumpet 187
Crumpet 62
Crunch Berry 82
Crystaline 158
Baby Cuddles 111, 180
Cuddles 74
Cuddly Cottontail 166
Cupcake 38
Curly Locks 71
Cutesaurus the Dinosaur 78
Cutie Calico 165

**D**

D.J. 92
Dabble 209
Daffodil 201
Dainty 105
Dainty Dahlia 98
Daisy 201
Daisy Dancer 114
Daisy Sweet 98
Dalmatian Dots 164
Baby Dancing Butterflies 213
Dancing Butterflies 67
Dangles 97
Princess Dawn 79
Dazzleglow 122, 123
Diamond Dreams 96
Dibbles 57
Dipper 61
Doodles 57
Baby Dots 'n Hearts 88
Dragon Suit and Sunsuit 228
Dream Castle 179, 195
Dream Gleamer 158
Dreamy Siamese 165
Baby Drummer 100
Duck Soup 178

**E**

Edgar the Elephant 78
Ember 36

**F**

Fair Flyer 160
Fancy Floppy 166
Fancy Flower 105
Baby Fifi 52
Fifi 38, 189
Baby Firefly 32, 110, 210
Firefly 23, 29, 122, 170, 173
Fizzy 43
Flashprance 221
Baby Fleecy 89
Baby Flicker 111
Floater 74, 151
Flowerbelle 133
Flower Bouquet 96
Flowerburst 105
Flower Darlings 230
Flower Dream 124
Flurry 107, 149
Flutterbye 31
Forget-Me-Not 45
Frilly Flower 106
From the Designer Collection 223
Baby Frosting 47
Funtime Spaniels 167

**G**

Galaxy 43
Galaxy Glamour 234
Baby Gametime 212
Gardenglow 124
Get Into The Groove 232
Gingerbread 43
Baby Glider 88
Glider 156
Glittering Gem 101
Baby Glory 33, 210
Glory 23, 30, 170, 173
Glow 81
Goldilocks 217
Baby Graffiti 77
Great Skates 220
Baby Gusty 41, 110
Gusty 29, 38

**H**

Baby Half Note 184, 211
Half Note 126
Happyglow 123
Happy Hopper 166
Happy Hugs 137
Happy Tabby 165
Having a Luau 223
Hearts and Candy 223
Baby Heart Throb 41
Heart Throb 29, 39
High Flier 81
High Tide 34
Hippity-Hop 39
Hit The Slopes 232

247

# The My Little Pony G1 Collector's Inventory

Holly 202
Hollywood 203
Home Sweet Home 194
Honeysuckle 45
Baby Hoppy the Kangaroo 90
Hula Hula 117
Hushabye 64

## I

Ice Princesses 230
In The Center Ring 234

## J

Jabber 75
Jangles 57
Jebber 75
Jumper and Snowsuit 228

## K

Kingsley the Lion 56
Kittens and Teddies 235

## L

Lady Flutter 81
Lady Labrador 164
Lavender Lace 98
Baby Leafy the Calf 90
Baby Leaper 100
Lemon Drop 177, 211
Lemon Treats 91
Li'l Cupcake 209
Li'l Pocket 124
Li'l Sweetcake 209
Li'l Tot 202
Baby Lickety-Split 41, 53, 171
Lickety-Split 28, 39, 171
Lights, Camera, Action 224
Lily 45
Lily of the Valley 201
Little Flitter 81, 149
Little Giggles 128
Little Honey Pie 128
Little Tabby 128
Little Whiskers 128
Locket 66
Baby Lofty 42, 171
Lofty 39, 171
Lovebeam 131
Baby Love Melody 213
Love Melody 67
Love Petal 133
Lovin' Kisses 137

Lucky, the Stallion 204
Baby Lucky Leaf 90
Lullabye Nursery 182

## M

Magic Hat 74
Magic Star 39, 152
Mainsail 104
Majesty 179, 211
Mane Waves 160
Masquerade 43
Mayfair 159
Medley 23, 29
Megan 30, 44, 95
Megan's Place 181
Merriweather 84
Merry Treat 110
Milk 'N Cookies 232
Milkweed 58
Baby Milky Way 213
Milky Way 67
Mimic 66
Mint Dreams 91
Minty 20, 203
Mirror Mirror 74
Misty 85, 150
Princess Misty 79
Molasses 91
Molly 49
Mommy 219
Baby Moondancer 33
Moondancer 23, 30, 170
Baby Moondreamer 210
Princess Moondust 79
Moon Jumper 107
Moonstone 24
Morning Glory 45, 157, 201
Munchy 84
My Pretty Pony 17, 18

## N

Napper 102, 207
Neon Lights 222
Nibbles 57
Nightcap 63
Night Glider 84
Baby Noddins 77
Noodles 57
Baby North Star 110
North Star 39
Baby Northstar 53

## O

Oakly the Moose 78

Overalls and Bunny Suit 228

## P

Pageant Queen 224
Baby Palm Tree 134
Parade Pizzazz 220
Paradise 39
Paradise Estate 185
Parasol 24, 172
Party Time 47, 221
Baby Paws 100
Peach Blossom 45
Peachy 18, 176
Baby Pearly 132
Peeks 75
Peppermint Crunch 82
Perky Persians 168
Perm Shoppe 188
Picnic in the Park 229
Pillow Talk 63
Piña Colada 117
Baby Pineapple 134
Pink Dreams 63, 65
Pinwheel 31
Player 92
Baby Pockets 90
Pom Pom Pony 222
Pony-Naut 233
Pony Bride 113
Pony Holiday 232
Pony Luv 222
Pony Purse 183, 187
Pony Royal 221
Pony Workout 225
Poof 'n Puff Perfume Palace 189
Poppy 201
Posey 28, 39, 169
Posey Rose 116
Powder 29
Precious Persian 165
Pretty As A Picture 231
Pretty Beat 126
Pretty Belle 114
Pretty Parlor 176
Pretty Poodle 164
Pretty Puff 127
Pretty Vision 71
Prima Ballerina 225
Princess Primrose 59
Princess Baby Buggy 196
Princess Pony (pink) 125
Princess Pony (purple) 125
Baby Princess Sparkle 196

Princess Pristina 79
Puddles 75, 148

## Q

Baby Quackers 53
Quackers 66
Quarterback 54

## R

Baby Racer 100
Raincurl 115
Baby Rainfeather 111
Baby Rainribbon 121
Rapunzel 217
Raspberry Jam 83
Rattles 58, 138
Ready for Rainbows 227
Red Roses 98
Baby Ribbon 42
Ribbon 40
Ribbons and Lace 235
Baby Ribbs 77
Ringlet 115
Ringlets 72
Ripple 46
Rock-a-Bye Bed 192
Rockin' The Night Away 233
Romper 73
Rose 201
Rosedust 45
Rosy Love 124
Princess Royal Blue 59
Ruby Lips 137

## S

Salty 54, 61
Sandcastle 76
Sand Digger 104
Sand Dollar 34
Satin 'n Lace 205
Satin Slipper Sweet Shoppe 187
Scoops 187
Scribbles 209
Scrub-A-Dub Spaniels 167
Scrub-a-Dub Tub 193
Scrumptious 40
Sea Breeze 34, 61, 117
Seaflower 104
Sealight 25, 85
Sea Mist 34
Baby Sea Princess 132
Seashell 22
Baby Sea Shimmer 132

# Index

Sea Shimmer  35, 46
Seashore  85, 235
Sea Spray  61
Sea Star  36
Seawinkle  25, 85
Secret Beauty  127
Secret Star  127
Princess Serena  59
Baby Shady  42
Shady  40
Shaggy  97
Sheertrimmer  160
Sherbet  82
Shoreline  104
Shovels  76
Show Stable  177
Sidewalk Surfer  231
Silky Slipper  116
Skippity-Doo  40
Sky Dancer  81
Skydancer  24
Skyflier  29, 156
Skylark  102
Sky Rocket  43, 102, 207
Sky Splasher  157
Baby Sleepie Pie  183
Sleep Tight  63
Sleepy Head  63
Slugger  54
Slumber Time Siamese  168
Sniffles  58, 76, 139
Baby Snippy  77
Baby Snookums  111
Snookums  58, 139
Snow Angels  227
Snowball  181
Snuzzle  20, 203
Baby Softsteps  120
Something Old, Something New  224
Song Rider  160
Songster  93
Princess Sparkle  60
Sparkler  30, 96
Speckles  76
Speedy  43
Spike  203
Spike the Dragon  179, 195
Splasher  36
Baby Splashes  88
Spring Song  106
Springy  131
Sprinkles  178, 211
Spritzy  161
Spunky the Camel  56

Squeezer  73
Squirmy  97
Baby Starbow  121
Baby Starburst  89
Princess Starburst  60
Star Dancer  103, 208
Stardazzle  127, 158
Starflash  112
Baby Starflower  110
Starflower  31
Star Gleamer  102
Starglow  123
Star Hopper  103, 208
Starry Wings  107
Starshine  24, 172
Starswirl  131
Steamer  54
Sticky  76
Baby Stockings  219
Strawberry Scoops  135
Strawberry Surprise  83
Streaky  115
Strike Up the Band  223
Baby Stripes  90
Stripes  115
Sudsy Angoras  168
Sugar Apple  91
Baby Sugarberry  213
Sugarberry  67
Baby Sugarcake  212
Sugar Sweet  91
Sun and Fun  226
Princess Sunbeam  80
Sunbeam  23, 136
Sunblossom  112
Baby Sundance  49
Sundance  30, 44, 95
Sunday Stroll  226
Sundrop  152
Sun Glider  107
Sunglory  136
Sunlight  24
Baby Sunnybunch  89
Sunnybunch  96
Baby Sunribbon  121
Sunshower  46
Sunsplasher  136
Sunspot  103, 208
Surf Rider  36, 46
Surfy  61
Baby Surprise  33, 171, 210
Surprise  30, 40, 171
Sweet Blossom  133
Sweet Celebrations Family  95

Sweet Dream Poodles  167
Sweet Dreams  65, 221, 231
Sweet Dreams Crib  193
Sweet Lily  99
Sweetness and Lace  224
Sweet Notes  126
Sweet Pocket  124
Sweet Pop  43
Sweet Scoops  216
Sweet Spaniel  164
Baby Sweetsteps  120
Baby Sweet Stuff  77
Sweet Stuff  44
Sweet Suds  99
Sweet Sundrop  114
Baby Sweet Tooth  213
Sweet Tooth  67
Swinger  93
Swirly Whirly  82

## T

Tabby  73, 150
Princess Taffeta  80
Taffy  62
Talk-A-Lot  139
Tall Tales  73
Tangles  57
Tap Dancer  93
Tappy  97
Tassles  96
Tattles  58, 138
Tex  54
The Tea Party  220
Tic-Tac-Toe  66
Tickle  31
Baby Tic Tac Toe  53
Baby Tiddly-Winks  182, 211
Princess Tiffany  60
Tiny Bubbles  36
Baby Tippytoes  120
Tip Toes  116
Baby Toe Dancer  120
Tootie Tails  117
Tootsie  28, 138
Topper  151
Toppy  75
Tossles  73
Trickles  31
Tropical Breeze  55
Truly  40
Tumbleweed  58
Tuneful  126
Tux 'n Tails  204
Twilight  23, 62

Twinkle Dancer  116
Twinkler  103, 112, 208
Twirler  93
Twist  40
Twisty Tail  72

## U

Baby Up, Up, and Away  213
Up, Up, and Away  67

## V

Violet  200

## W

Baby Waddles  101
Waterfall  178
Water Lily  46, 201
Wavedancer  25, 85
Wave Jumper  35
Wave Runner  104
Wavy  61
Whirly  107, 151
Baby Whirly-Twirl  77
Whitecap  35
Whizzer  44
Wiggles  97
Wig Wam  70
Wild Flower  106
Wind Drifter  55
Windsweeper  157
Wind Walker  156
Wind Whistler  40
Windy  24, 74, 172
Wingsong  55
Baby Woolley the Lamb  89
Woosie  73

## X

## Y

Yo-Yo  97
Yum Yum  47, 84

## Z

Zig Zag the Zebra  56

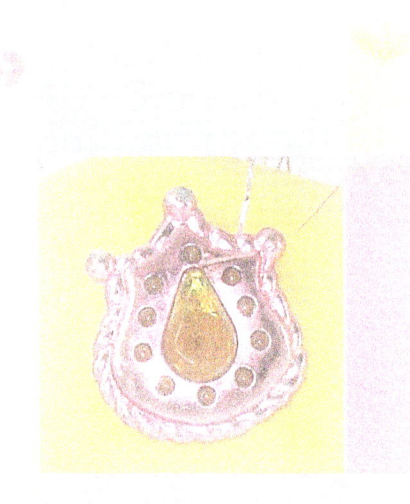

For more full color illustrated price guides to your favorite vintage toys, please visit us online at

http://www.collectorsinventory.com

~*~*~*~*~*~*~*~

## Also by Summer Hayes

### *The My Little Pony G2 Collector's Inventory*
*a full color illustrated price guide to all ponies, playsets and accessories released from 1997 to 2003*

### The My Little Pony G3 Collector's Inventory
*a full color illustrated guide to the third generation of MLP including all ponies, playsets and accessories released from 2003 to 2006*

### The My Little Pony G3 Collector's Inventory Part II
*a full color illustrated guide to all ponies, playsets and accessories released from 2006 through 2008*

For copies or more information about any of the My Little Pony Collector's Inventory titles, please visit:

http://www.mylittleponycollecting.com

www.ingramcontent.com/pod-product-compliance
Lightning Source LLC
Chambersburg PA
CBHW061210230426
43665CB00032B/2976